40.°°

AC0002

AC0010

AC0030

ABANDON CAST-OFF DEBRIS DECAY DECOMPOSED DELETE DEMOLISHED DESTROYED DETRITUS DISCARD

AC0039

AC0040

AC0052

AC0054

DISMANTLE DISPERSE DISPOSABLE DISRUPT DISSOLVE EJECTED ERASE EXPELLED EROSION

THANKS TO:

> LEONARDO BONANNI, DAVID MAGID, PAUL SCHUETTE, DAMEN HAMILTON, ALESSANDRO FARINELLA, THOMAS CHIROUSE, NICOLE JANKE, PAUL SAMALA, BETHANY KOBY, FRANCESCA ROATTA, PERNILLE BISGAARD, STEVEN HO, BRENT BUCK, MAGGIE PENG, RUTH RON, AND TAMI LEVINE FOR SHARING LONG HOURS WITH US AT LOT/EK WITH TOTAL COMMITMENT AND SUPPORT.
> JOHN HARTMANN, FOR SHOWING UP AT THE RIGHT TIME AND HELPING US TURN LOT/EK INTO AN "ARCHITECTURE OFFICE" WITH HIS ENERGY, THOUGHTFULNESS, AND TALENT.
> RICHARD MASSEY (ALIAS MR. MAN), FOR THIS BEAUTIFUL BOOK, FOR HIS PATIENCE IN THE LONG DAYS WE SPENT TOGETHER, FOR THE PLEASURE OF THE LATE BIG BIRD, AND THE DISCOVERY OF THE HAMBURGER CANDIES.
> MARK LAMSTER (ALIAS DADDY), FOR ENVISIONING A LOT/EK BOOK AND FOR ENDURING THE TORMENTS WE PUT HIM THROUGH.
> HENRY URBACH, FOR OUR SHARED DREAMS, HARDSHIPS, AND SUCCESSES.
> MAYER RUS, FOR MAKING US AS POPULAR AS YUL ULU.
> DAVID LEIBER, SIMON DOONAN, ELIZABETH SVERBEYEFF BYRON, JEFFREY DEITCH, RYOTA TANABE, KERRY MACINTOSH, AND LARRY RINDER, FOR BELIEVING IN US WHEN EVERYBODY ELSE THOUGHT WE WERE CRAZY.
> PETER GARAFANO, FOR SEEING OUR PRODUCTIONS AS A FUN BREAK IN HIS EVERYDAY ROUTINE AND PUTTING UP WITH US.
> MARC GANZGLASS, JAN HILMER, AARON DAVIDSON & MELISSA DUBBIN, AND ANN & TOM GUINEY FOR LENDING THEIR ART AND KNOWLEDGE TO THE EXECUTION OF OUR VISION.
> PAUL WARCHOL, FOR HIS WONDERFUL PHOTOGRAPHY AND HIS GENEROSITY.
> ADRIANA CUTOLO, FOR A BEAUTIFUL WEBSITE, WWW.LOT-EK.COM.
> DEIRDRE HOLLMAN & SHERRI WOLF, FOR HELPING US WORD THE UNWORDABLE.
> CAMPBELL HYERS AND HIS CREW, FOR GUIDING US THROUGH THE OBSCURITY OF COMPUTER NETWORKING.
> JAMES ORTENZIO, FOR BEING OUR GUARDIAN ANGEL.
> ALESSANDRA ALECCI, LORRAINE KESSLER, JACQUELINE & STEVE FRANKEL, CONNIE HANSEN & RUSSELL PEACOCK (GUZMAN), STEVEN MILLER & CHRISTINE JONES, JASON PICKLEMAN, DAVID LEVINE, FRANCINE HERMELIN AND ADAM LEVITE, JOSH MORTON, GGRIPPO, SARA MELTZER & ADAM AMES, AMY CAPPELLAZZO & JOANNE ROSEN, MASSIMILIANO DI BATTISTA & MARCO FINCATO, PIERANTONIO GIACOPPO & ANTHONY IANNACCI, IAN KWOON, PAOLA ANTONELLI, TOM HEALY AND FRED HOCHBERG, LISA PHILLIPS AND EVERYBODY AT THE NEW MUSEUM, KURT KIEFER, AND FRED HENRY, FOR GIVING US THE OPPORTUNITY TO DEVELOP OUR VISION THROUGH SUCH EXCITING PROJECTS.
> AMY BERNSTEIN, MAURICE RUSSELL, RON NORSWORTHY, ISABEL GOUVERNEUR, JANEIL ENGELSTAD, ALEX & LAURA STOJANOVIC, FOR HELPING US THROUGH OUR UPS AND DOWNS.
> JONATHAN & DANNY, FOR THEIR LOVE.
> MASINA, PAOLO AND PASQUALE, TINA, MARIO, AND MARIA PAOLA, FOR THEIR UNQUESTIONING LIFETIME SUPPORT.
> NONNA ADA AND NONNA LUCREZIA, FOR MAKING EVERYTHING ALL RIGHT (EVEN WHEN IT ISN'T!).

IN THIS PROTOTYPE FOR A SHIPPABLE AMERICAN DINER, TWO SEA CONTAINERS ARE COUPLED LEAVING A GAP IN BETWEEN.

CUTS IN THE CORRUGATED METAL SKIN OF THE CONTAINERS CREATE LONG HORIZONTAL WINDOWS ALONG THEIR SIDES.

THE RESTAURANT NAME—AMERICAN DINER #1—IS PRINTED WITH FLUORESCENT PAINT ON THE OUTSIDE, AND RUNS AROUND THE ENTIRE VOLUME, TURNING THE BUILDING INTO ITS OWN THREE-DIMENSIONAL SIGN.

4   ONE CONTAINER SERVES AS THE DINING ROOM, WHILE THE OTHER HOUSES THE KITCHEN, ENTRANCE, AND RESTROOMS.

A ROW OF STOOLS RUNS ALONG THE EDGE OF THE DINING CONTAINER FACING A LONG COUNTER THAT JUTS OUT OF THE OPPOSITE KITCHEN CONTAINER.

SUNLIGHT POURS ONTO THE COUNTER THROUGH THE SPACE BETWEEN THE TWO CONTAINERS, WHICH IS SEALED WITH GLASS.

THE CONTAINERS WILL BE FULLY CONVERTED AND FURNISHED IN THE UNITED STATES AND THEN SHIPPED TO JAPAN FOR INSTALLATION.

THEIR MODULARITY ALLOWS FOR MULTIPLE CONFIGURATIONS.

EXPLODE FRACTION FRAGMENT LEFT LEFTOVER MUTILATED NEGLECTED OBSOLETE PARTIAL PORTION REFUSE REJECTED RESIDUE SCRAP SEDIMENT SEGMENT SURPLUS TRASH

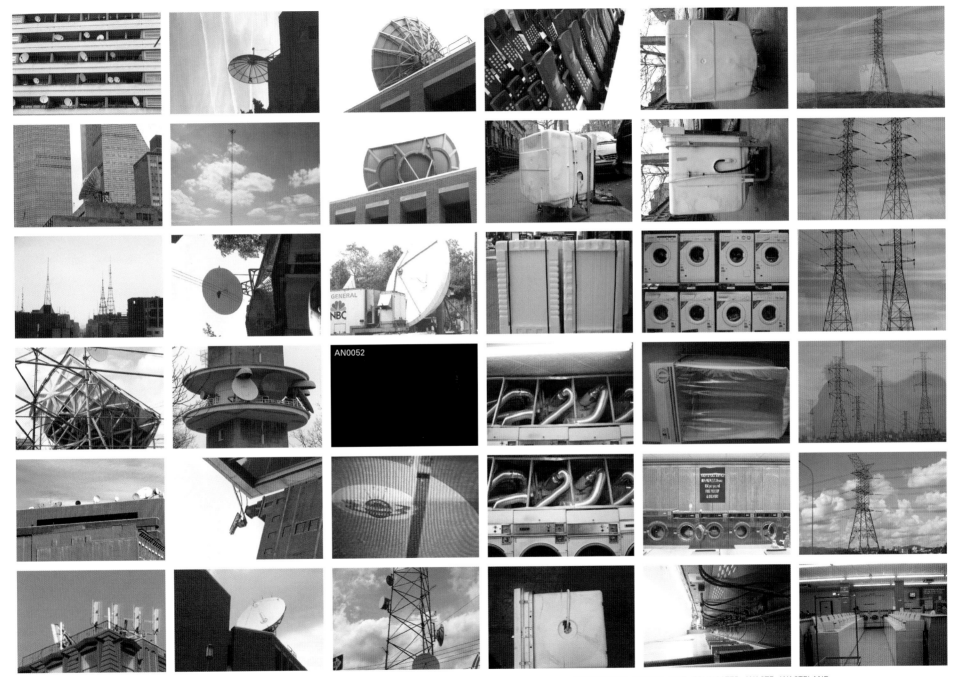

AN0052

THROWAWAY THROW OUT TRUNCATED WASTE WASTELAND

BAM 96 97 98
TEMPORARY ENVIRONMENTS FOR THE BROOKLYN ACADEMY OF
MUSIC NEXT WAVE FESTIVAL OPENING GALAS
BROOKLYN, NY, 1996–98

BAM 96
IN THIS ORWELLIAN REFECTORY, SPACE IS DEFINED
THROUGH THE AXIAL REPETITION OF TELEVISED IMAGES THAT
BREAK THROUGH A NIGHTLIKE ATMOSPHERE.

TABLES ARE PAIRED AND SEPARATED BY A 12-INCH GAP.
TELEVISION SETS ARE CLAMPED FACE UP ALONG THIS GAP,
INTRODUCING "SIMULATED GUESTS" ON SCREENS AT THE
TABLES.

FLUORESCENT-TAPE NOTCHES MARK THE SEATING ARRANGEMENT, WHILE LETTERS AND NUMBERS CODE THE TABLE LAYOUT, GENERATING AN ATMOSPHERE REMINISCENT OF THE VIEW OF AN AIRPORT RUNWAY DURING A NIGHT LANDING.

TOILETS

BAR

DANCE

ENTER

SRVC

SERVICE ENTRANCE

IN THIS TIMEPORT, STREAMING PERSPECTIVES INDUCE THE VIRTUAL EXPERIENCE OF LIGHT-SPEED ACCELERATION AND TIME TRAVEL.

STRAIGHT LINES OF BLUE LIGHT SHOOT BETWEEN ROWS OF COLUMNS, FORMING A DENSE BLUE ATMOSPHERE IN AN OTHERWISE WHITE WAREHOUSE SPACE.

AT THE FOCAL POINT OF THESE VECTORS, GIANT DIGITAL DISPLAYS CLOCK THE ANNUAL PROGRESSION OF TIME INTO THE FUTURE. A CONTINUOUS LINE OF BLUE FLUORESCENT TUBES BISECTS THE TABLES, CONNECTING THEM IN A FISHBONE PATTERN.

11 THE DINERS ARE SEATED ON EITHER SIDE OF THE LUMINOUS AISLE.
THE TUBES RESTING ON THE TABLETOPS MIRROR THE
FLUORESCENT FIXTURES THAT HANG FROM THE CEILING AND
APPEAR LIKE RAILS FOR VIRTUAL MOVEMENT.

BAM 98
AN INTIMATE, ILLUMINATED CORE IS DEFINED WITHIN A LARGE
INDUSTRIAL SHED.

MADE FROM A MILKY TARP, THE CORE FORMS A CORRIDORLIKE SPACE APPROXIMATELY 30 FEET WIDE, 20 FEET HIGH, AND 230 FEET LONG. TELEVISION IMAGES ARE REAR PROJECTED ONTO THESE PLASTIC WALLS.

THE LARGE MOVING IMAGES DEMATERIALIZE THIS ENCLOSURE, WHICH IS INHABITED BY DINERS SEATED ALONG THREE 200-FOOT-LONG TABLES.

BILLBOARDS

ABERRANT ABNORMAL

ABSTRUSE ABSURD ALIEN ANOMALY BLUR CACOPHONY CICATRIX CONTORT CRACK CRASHED DEFECTIVE DEFORM DENT DISSONANCE DISTURBANCE

DISTORTION FAULTY FLAW HICCUP HYBRID INCLINE INCOMPATIBLE INCONGRUOUS INSTABILITY INTRICATE JAGGED KITSCH LESION LISP

BB0083

BB0113

BOHEN FOUNDATION
CONTEMPORARY ART FOUNDATION
NEW YORK 2001

THE BOHEN FOUNDATION SUPPORTS CONTEMPORARY ART AND
CULTURE, COMMISSIONING AND EXHIBITING WORKS OF A SCALE
AND COMPLEXITY THAT DO NOT LEND THEMSELVES TO THE
CONTEXT OF A NORMAL GALLERY.

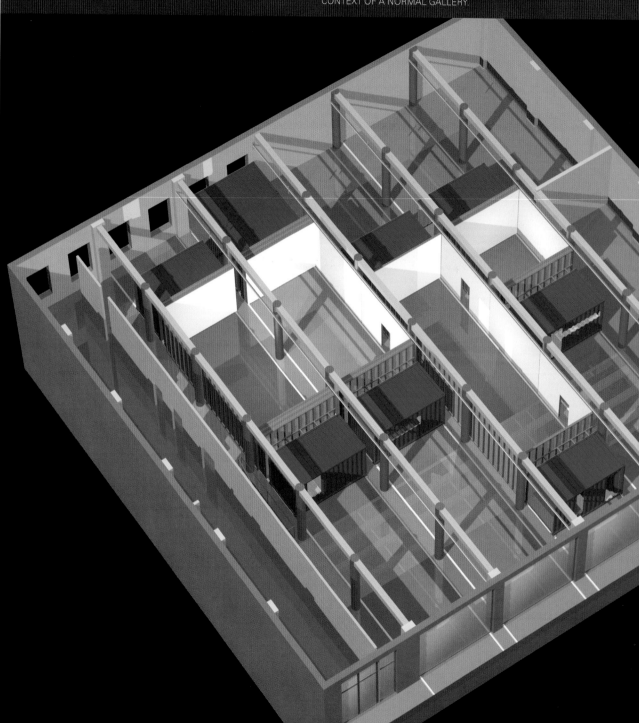

ITS OPERATION REQUIRES MAXIMUM SPATIAL FLEXIBILITY TO ALLOW THE EXHIBITION OF DIFFERENT MEDIA, FROM DRAWINGS AND PAINTINGS TO PROJECTIONS, SCULPTURAL OBJECTS, SITE-SPECIFIC WORKS, AND MULTIMEDIA INSTALLATIONS.

TWELVE SHIPPING CONTAINER SECTIONS ARE INTRODUCED WITHIN THE SQUARE STRUCTURAL GRID OF THE GROUND FLOOR AND THE BASEMENT OF A FORMER PRINTING FACILITY.

EACH CONTAINER SECTION IS A MOVABLE ENCLOSURE AND ALSO CARRIES FIVE 15-X-12-FOOT FOLDABLE WALL PANELS THAT ARE PACKED ON THE CONTAINER'S SIDE.

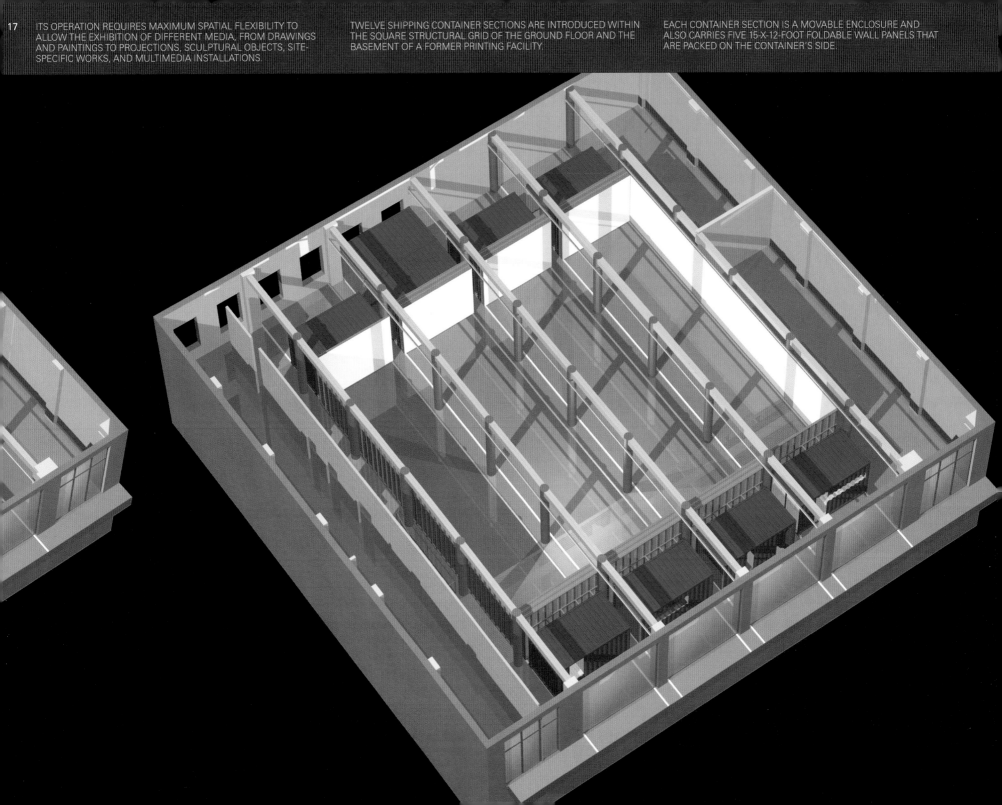

18 ON THE GROUND FLOOR, TWO CONTAINER SECTIONS ARE POSITIONED WITHIN EACH BAY, GENERATING EXHIBITION SPACES BY SLIDING ALONG TRACKS TO PRESET LOCATIONS.

ONCE THEY ARE MOVED INTO POSITION, THE WALL PANELS ARE UNFOLDED TO FORM THE EXHIBITION SPACES. THE MODULARITY OF THE WALL PANELS ALLOWS FOR THESE SPACES TO TAKE ON VARIOUS SIZES AND SHAPES ACCORDING TO CURATORIAL NEEDS.

A LONG SECTION OF THE GROUND FLOOR IS CUT OUT AND COVERED WITH A REMOVABLE METAL GRID. CONTAINER SECTIONS AND THEIR WALL PANELS CAN BE ALIGNED ALONG SUCH FLOOR OPENINGS TO CREATE DOUBLE-HEIGHT EXHIBITION SPACES. ALONG WITH THE

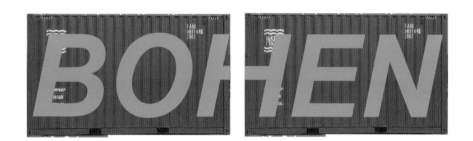

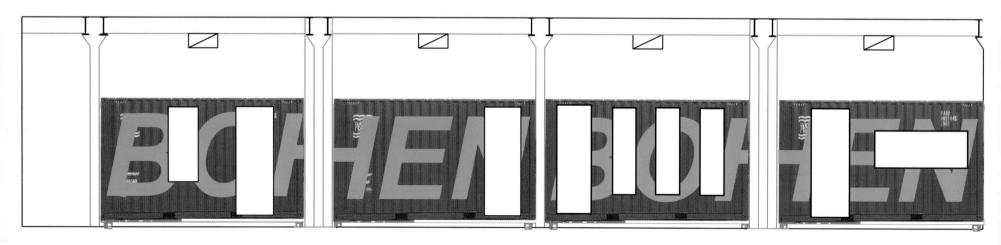

FLEXIBILITY OF THE SPATIAL ORGANIZATION. THIS SYSTEM CREATES A STRONG VISUAL DISTINCTION BETWEEN THE SMOOTH WHITE INTERIOR OF THE EXHIBITION AREAS AND THE UNFINISHED WAREHOUSE SPACE.

THE CONTAINER SECTIONS HOUSE A VARIETY OF ENCLOSED FUNCTIONS: OFFICE, LOUNGE, A BOOK AND VIDEO LIBRARY, AND A CONFERENCE ROOM.

THE BASIC FURNITURE WITHIN EACH CONTAINER IS CUT AND BENT OUT OF THE CONTAINER SKIN ITSELF. THE RESULTING PLANES ARE LAYERED WITH CLEAR RESIN, FOAM, OR RUBBER TO BE TRANSFORMED INTO DESKS, BENCHES, AND SHELVES.

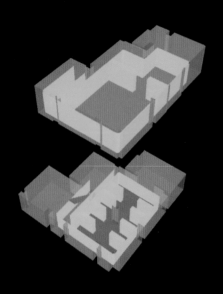

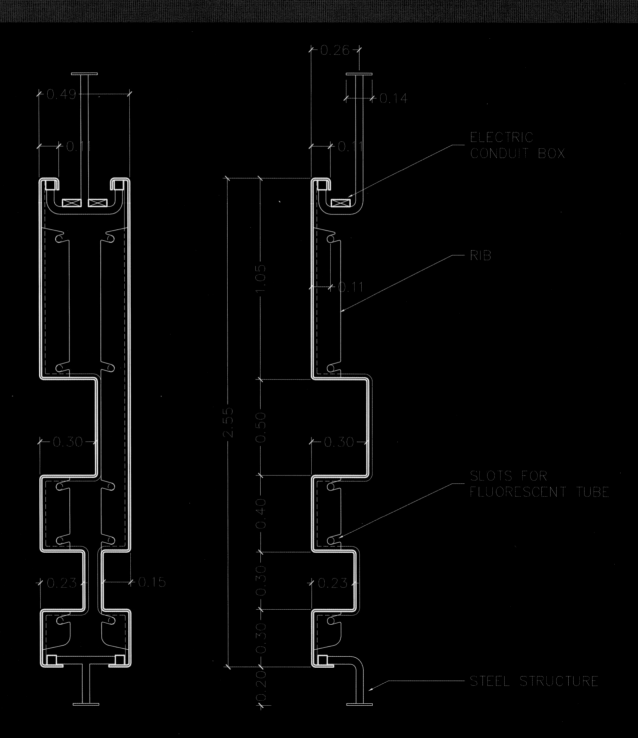

ELECTRIC
CONDUIT BOX

RIB

SLOTS FOR
FLUORESCENT TUBE

STEEL STRUCTURE

THE BAND, SUPPORTED FROM BEHIND BY A STEEL-PIPE FRAME, FLOATS IN THE SPACE WITHOUT TOUCHING THE FLOOR OR THE CEILING, LEAVING THE EXISTING SHELL IN ITS UNFINISHED STATE.

THE BAND'S PANELS ARE CONTOURED TO CREATE A LOW, NARROW COMPARTMENT FOR SHOES AND A LARGE UPPER ONE FOR BAGS AND OTHER ACCESSORIES.

AS THE PANELS ARE INSTALLED, THEIR COMPARTMENTS FORM TWO CONTINUOUS GROOVES THAT ACT AS TRACKS FOR A SERIES OF ROLLING WALLS.

↙ DOWN TO SHOP

THESE WALLS BREAK UP THE SPACE ON BOTH FLOORS, CREATING TWO DISTINCT EXHIBITION AREAS ON THE UPPER LEVEL AND INDIVIDUAL BAYS FOR EACH DESIGNER ON THE LOWER.

GELS CAN BE INSTALLED AROUND THE FLUORESCENT TUBES
TO CHANGE THE COLOR OF PART OR ALL OF THE ENVIRONMENT.

MALFUNCTION OBSCENE ODD OUT-OF-FOCUS OUT-OF-PLUMB PECULIARITY PRIMITIVE SCAR STRIDENT TASTELESS UNCANNY UNCOMMON UNFAMILIAR UNNATURAL UNUSUAL WARPED WEIRD

BO0030

ABRUPT ALTERNATING BRIEF CHANGEABLE CYCLIC DISCONTINUOUS EPHEMERAL EXPIRED EVANESCENT IMMEDIATE

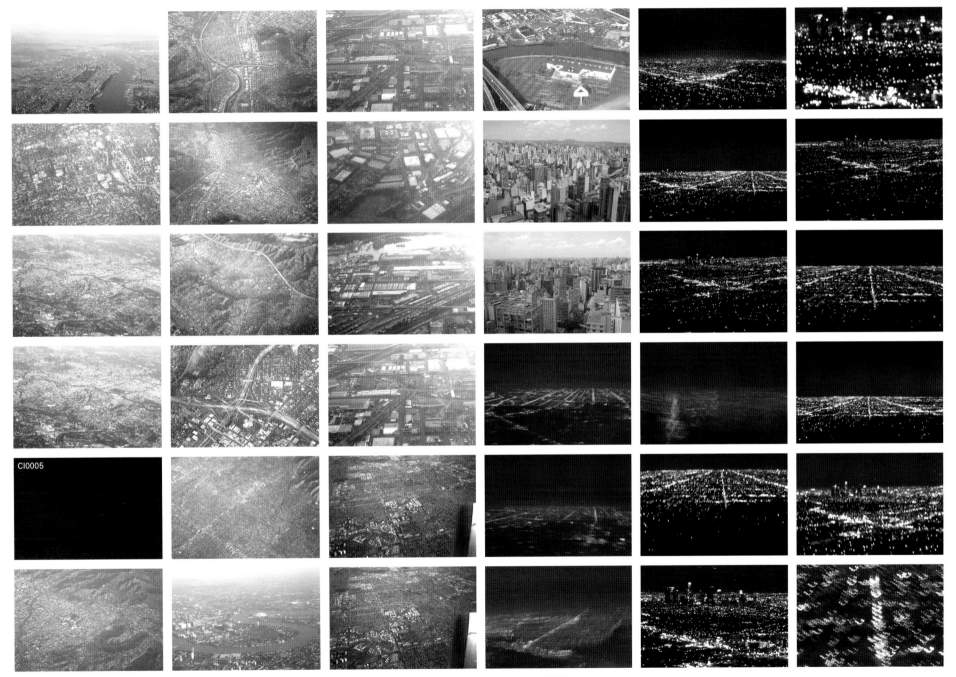

CI0005

IMPERMANENT INCOMPLETE INCONSTANT IN-PROGRESS INSTANT INSTANTANEOUSLY INTERIM INTERMITTENT

INTERRUPTED MOMENTARY NOW ONGOING PHASE PRESENT PROP-UP

RECURRENT SUDDEN TEMPORARY TRANSIENT TRANSITORY UNFINISHED VARIABLE VANISHING

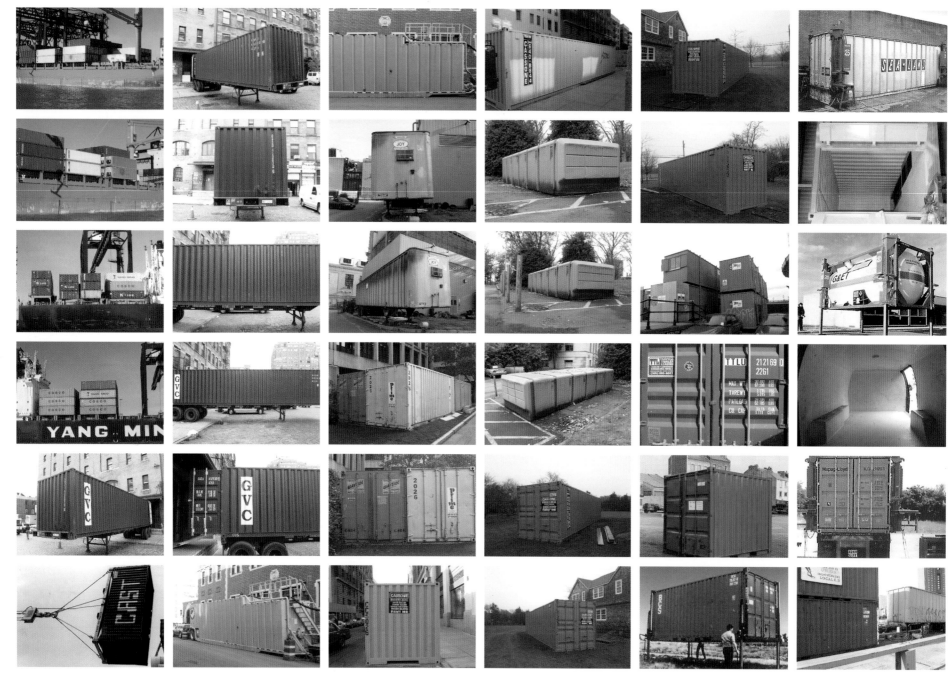

ABSENCE ALL-PURPOSE AMNESIA BALD BANAL BARE BASIC BLANK CARELESS COMMON DESERT EMPTY EXPOSED FACELESS GENERIC INDEFINITE INSTITUTIONAL LACK LESS MARGINAL NAKED NAMELESS

CO0076

CO0090

CO0091

CO0092

NAMELESS NONDESCRIPT NOTHINGNESS NOWHERE NUDE OBVIOUS OFF ORDINARY RAW REVEAL SCATTERED

SECONDARY SPARSE SPORADIC STRIPPED TRANSPARENT UNCLASSIFIED UNINHABITED UNREFINED

CR0010B

UNSOPHISTICATED UTILITARIAN VACANT VACUUM VAGUE VERSATILE VOID ZERO

ABSORB ACCUMULATE ADD-ON ADHERE ADOPT ALIEN ANNEX ACQUIRE AMASS ASSIMILATE BURY

PUBLISHED BY
PRINCETON ARCHITECTURAL PRESS
37 EAST SEVENTH STREET
NEW YORK, NEW YORK 10003

©2002 PRINCETON ARCHITECTURAL PRESS
ALL RIGHTS RESERVED
PRINTED IN CHINA
04 03 02 01   5 4 3 2 1 FIRST EDITION

NO PART OF THIS BOOK MAY BE USED OR REPRODUCED IN ANY
MANNER WITHOUT WRITTEN PERMISSION FROM THE PUBLISHER,
EXCEPT IN THE CONTEXT OF REVIEWS.

EVERY REASONABLE ATTEMPT HAS BEEN MADE TO IDENTIFY
OWNERS OF COPYRIGHT. ERRORS OR OMISSIONS WILL BE
CORRECTED IN SUBSEQUENT EDITIONS.

EDITOR MARK LAMSTER
DESIGN RICHARD MASSEY AT O.I.G

*SPECIAL THANKS TO: NETTIE ALJIAN, ANN ALTER, AMANDA ATKINS,
NICOLA BEDNAREK, JANET BEHNING, PENNY CHU, JAN CIGLIANO,
JANE GARVIE, TOM HUTTEN, CLARE JACOBSON, NANCY EKLUND
LATER, LINDA LEE, ANNE NITSCHKE, EVAN SCHONINGER, LOTTCHEN
SHIVERS, JENNIFER THOMPSON, AND DEB WOOD OF PRINCETON
ARCHITECTURAL PRESS*
—KEVIN C. LIPPERT, PUBLISHER

LIBRARY OF CONGRESS CATALOGING-IN-PUBLICATION DATA
TOLLA, ADA;
URBAN SCAN / LOT/EK [AUTHORS, ADA TOLLA, GIUSEPPE LIGNANO] ;
P.   CM.
ISBN 1-56898-300-X
1. LOT/EK ARCHITECTURE.
2. ARCHITECTURE—UNITED STATES—20TH CENTURY.
I. LIGNANO, GIUSEPPE. II. TITLE.
NA737.L68 A4 2002
720'.92'2—DC21
2001005546

FOR A FREE CATALOG OF BOOKS, CALL 1.800.722.6657, OR VISIT OUR
WEB SITE AT WWW.PAPRESS.COM.

THE PROGRAM FOR THE TRANSFORMATION OF THIS INDUSTRIAL
BUILDING IN SOHO CALLED FOR A LARGE GALLERY SPACE, A PUBLIC
LOBBY WITH A CAFE, AND A STORAGE AREA WITH A SMALLER
PRIVATE SHOWROOM.

A VAST VOID IS ENCLOSED IN THE CENTER OF THE SPACE, WITH SHIPPING CONTAINERS WEDGED BETWEEN THIS VOID AND THE PERIMETER WALLS OF THE EXISTING BUILDING.

A CONTINUOUS WHITE BAND THAT WRAPS COMPLETELY AROUND THE SPACE AND IS DETACHED FROM THE BUILDING'S WALLS DEFINES THE VOID.

THE CONTAINERS BREAK THROUGH THE BUILDING'S FRONT FACADE WHERE THEY RANDOMLY OVERLAP WITH THE EXISTING DOORS AND WINDOWS AS THEY PUNCH THROUGH TO THE OUTSIDE.

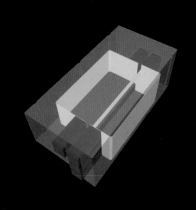

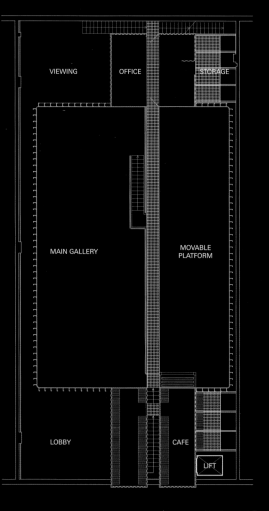

VIEWING OFFICE STORAGE

MAIN GALLERY MOVABLE PLATFORM

LOBBY CAFE

LIFT

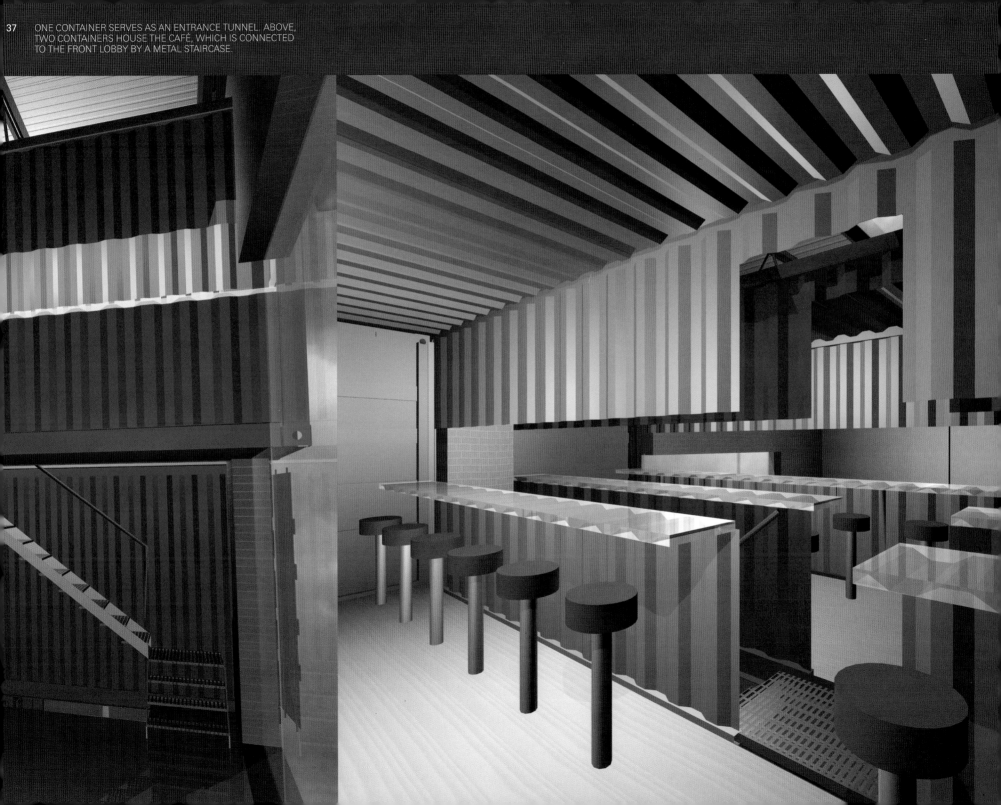

ONE CONTAINER SERVES AS AN ENTRANCE TUNNEL. ABOVE,
TWO CONTAINERS HOUSE THE CAFÉ, WHICH IS CONNECTED
TO THE FRONT LOBBY BY A METAL STAIRCASE.

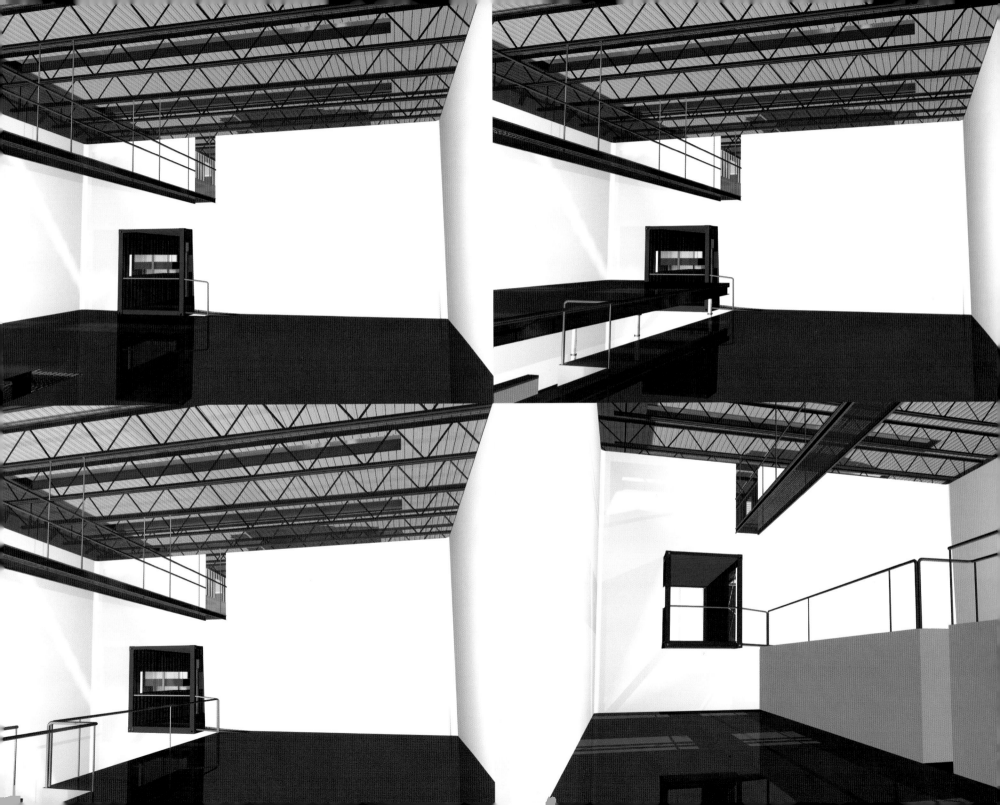

IN THE BACK, SUSPENDED OVER THE STORAGE / SHOWROOM AREA, THE CONTAINERS HOUSE A PRIVATE OFFICE.

FASHIONLAB
BROOKLYN, NY, 1999
FASHION EVENT

ON A VAST WAREHOUSE FLOOR, BLUE SHRINK-WRAP IS STRETCHED
BETWEEN COLUMNS IN A RANDOM ZIGZAG PATTERN.

FLUORESCENT TUBES, ATTACHED TO THE COLUMNS, DIFFUSE A
DENSE BLUE LIGHT THROUGH THE COLORED SHRINK-WRAP.
GLOWING ORANGE LINES ON THE FLOOR GUIDE VISITORS THROUGH
THE LABYRINTH.

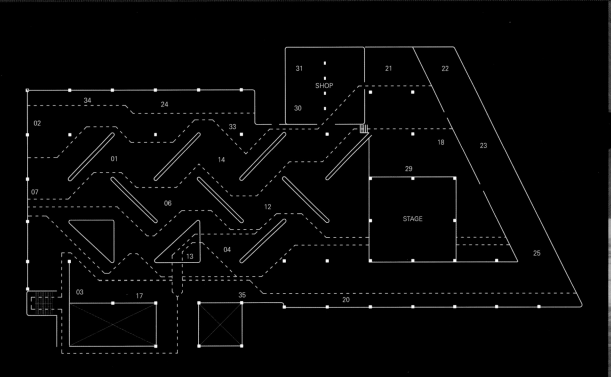

CLIMB CLING CONTAGIOUS CONTAMINATE EMBED EMBODY ENCAPSULATE ENCLOSE

PANORAMA, *MID-ATLANTIC*, FROM ALLAN SEKULA, *FISH STORY*, 1995

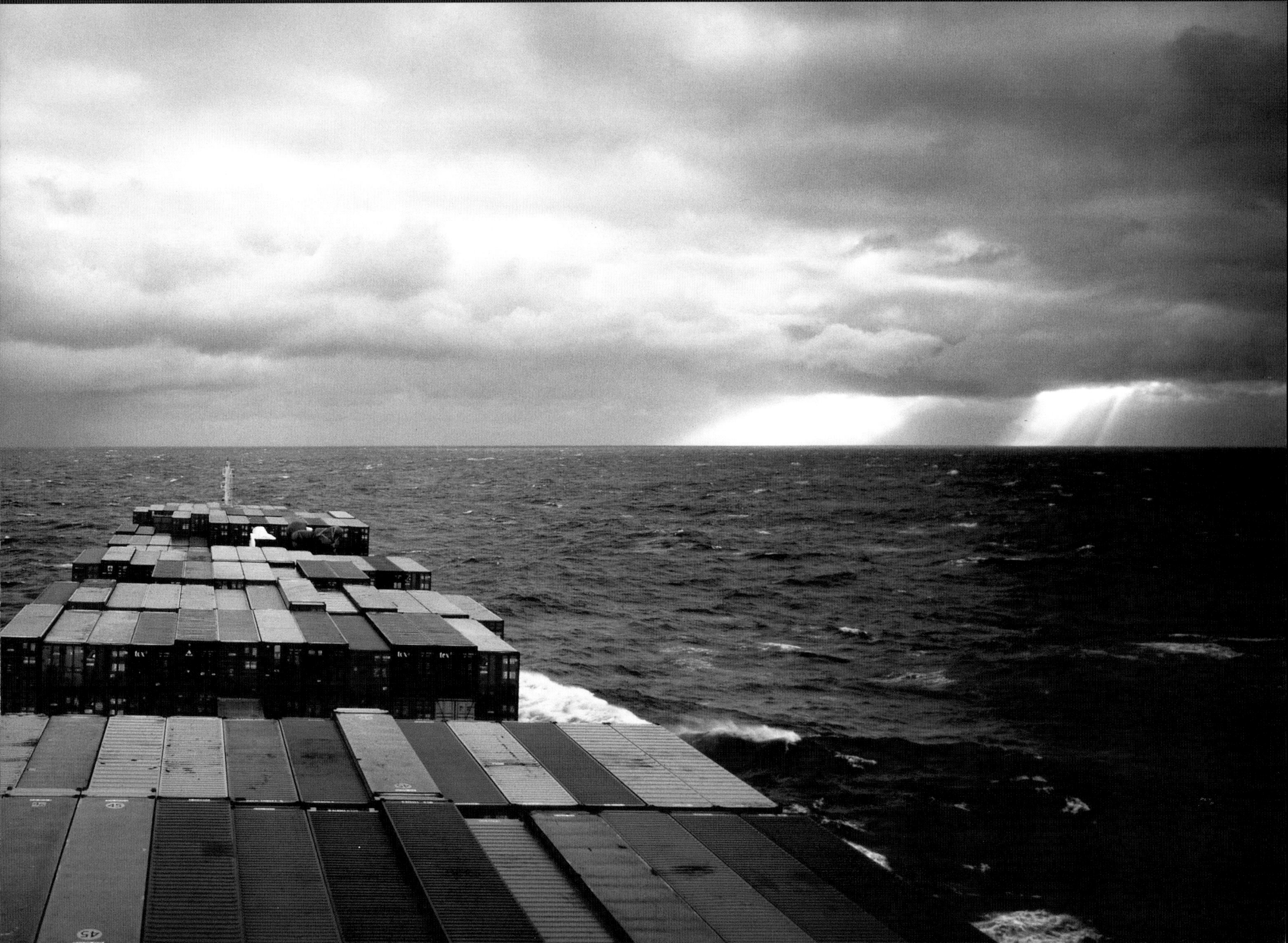

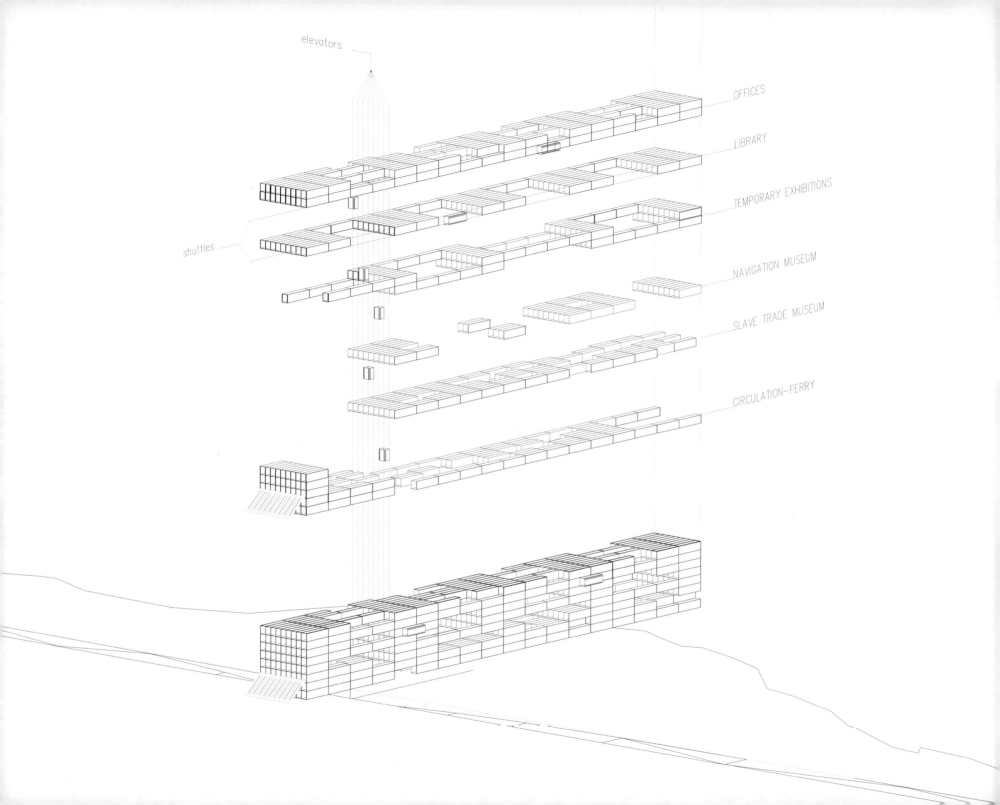

elevators

OFFICES

LIBRARY

TEMPORARY EXHIBITIONS

shuttles

NAVIGATION MUSEUM

SLAVE TRADE MUSEUM

CIRCULATION-FERRY

A SINGLE ARCHITECTURAL CONCEPT REPRESENTS THE BRUTALITY OF THE SLAVE TRADE AND THE EXCITEMENT OF TRANS-ATLANTIC EXPLORATION.

THE STRUCTURE, A MONOLITHIC ELEMENT SUSPENDED BETWEEN EARTH AND WATER, IS ENTIRELY MADE OF SHIPPING CONTAINERS.

JUTTING OUT INTO THE OCEAN OR PENETRATING INTO THE LAND, IT IS A TRUNCATED LINK BETWEEN AFRICA AND THE AMERICAS.

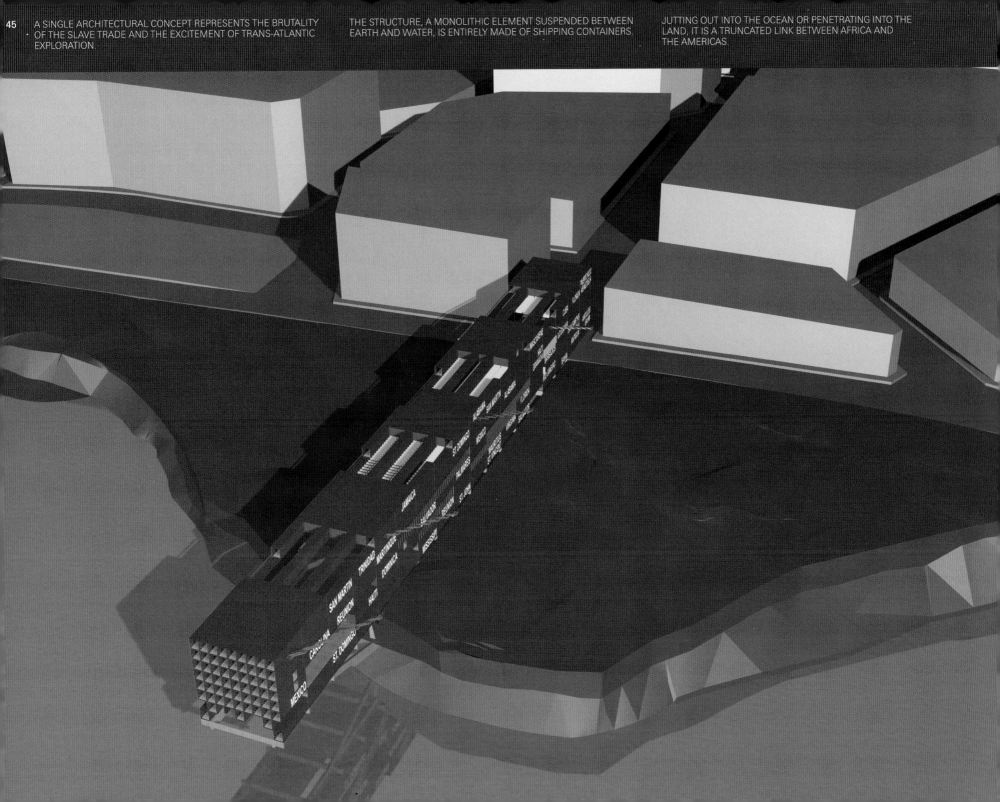

THE BUILDING IS DESIGNED TO ACHIEVE A MONUMENTAL VALUE. AT A TERRITORIAL SCALE, IT MARKS THE EARTH/WATER EDGE AT THE WESTERNMOST POINT IN AFRICA. AT THE URBAN SCALE, IT INTRUDES INTO THE FABRIC OF DAKAR FROM THE OCEAN.

AT A MORE EXPERIENTIAL LEVEL, IT TAKES VISITORS ON PATHS THROUGH SPACES THAT MODULATE THE INTENSITY OF THEIR EXPERIENCE.

AS A SELF-SUPPORTING MODULAR ELEMENT, IT HAS BEEN PIERCED, STACKED, AND COMBINED TO MEET THE FUNCTIONAL REQUIREMENTS OF THE PROGRAM.

LAYERS OF THESE CONTAINERS, CORRESPONDING TO LAYERS OF FUNCTIONS, INTERLOCK WITH ONE ANOTHER TO FORM A SELF-CONTAINED HORIZONTAL PRISM. THE EXPERIENCE OF THE SLAVE TRADE MUSEUM IS AT ONCE SPATIAL AND EMOTIONAL.

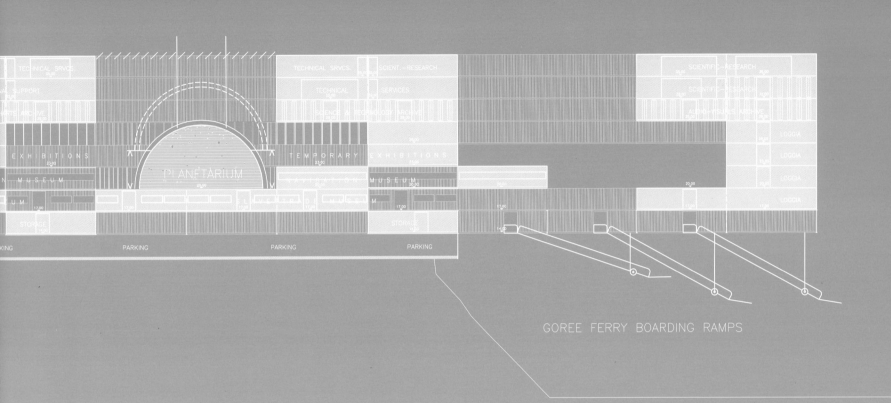

GOREE FERRY BOARDING RAMPS

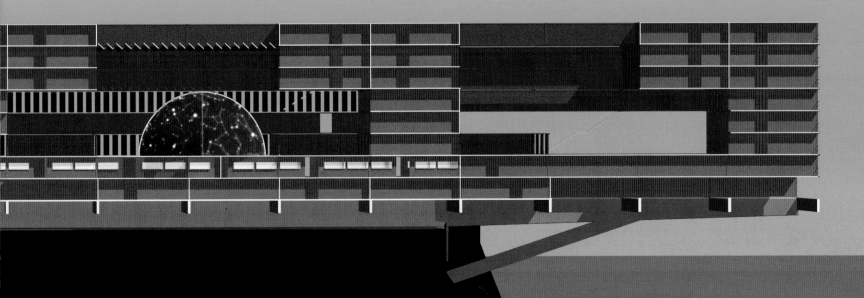

PLACED IN THE LOWER PART OF THE BUILDING, ITS LABYRINTHINE LAYOUT, WITH A SUCCESSION OF FRAGMENTED CORRIDORS AND SMALL HALLS, EMULATES THE HOLD OF A SHIP.

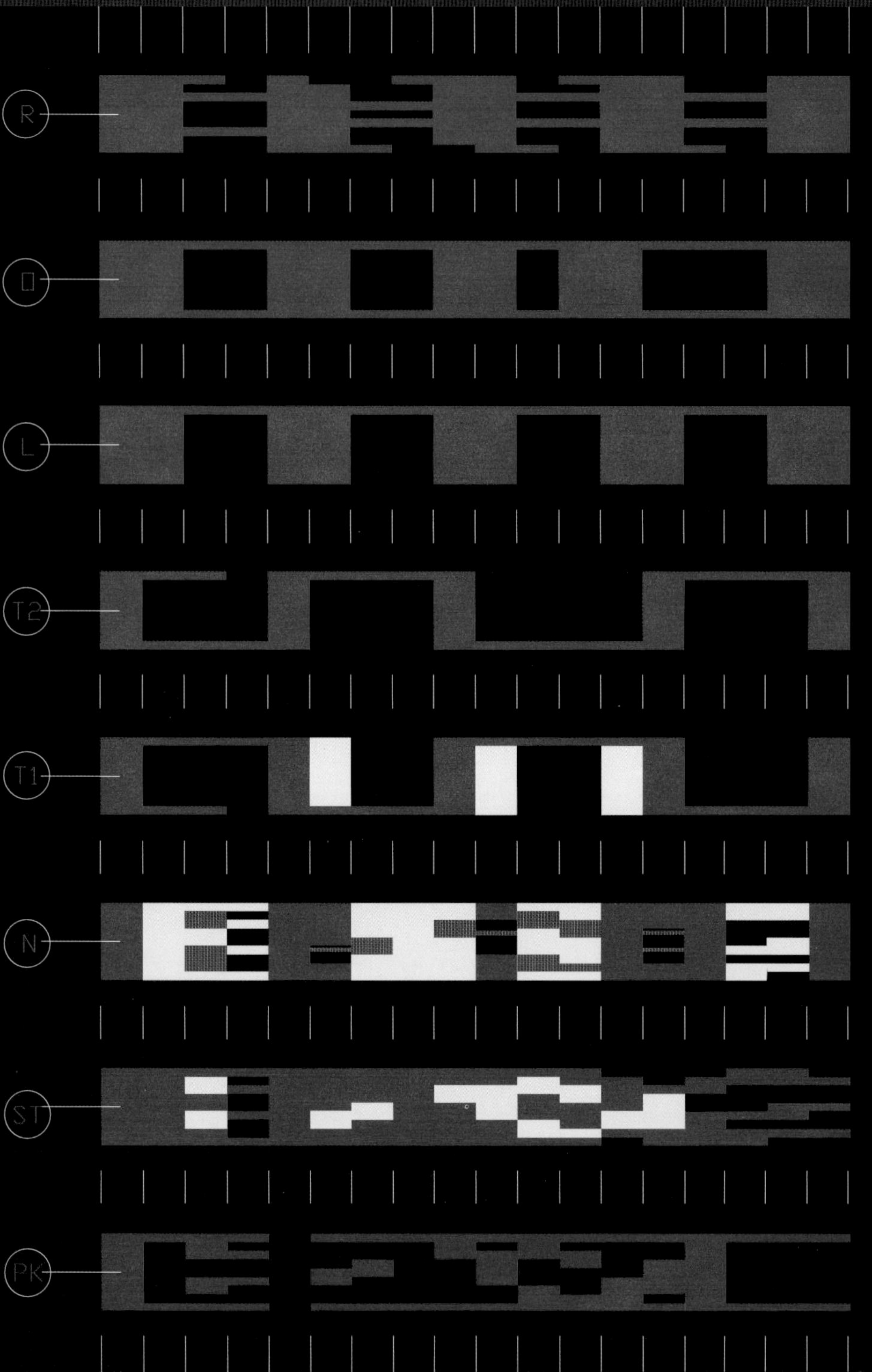

THE CONTAINERS ARE PIERCED FOR CROSS CIRCULATION AND ILLUMINATION, AND FURNISHED WITH GLASS SHOWCASES IMBEDDED IN THEIR SIDES.

THE NAVIGATION MUSEUM, ON THE LAYER IMMEDIATELY ABOVE, IS ENTERED VIA PARALLEL CORRIDORS THAT OPEN UP INTO LARGE HALLS WHERE OPENINGS REVEAL THE SIGHT OF LAND, OCEAN, AND SKY.

THE FOUR LAYERS ABOVE, WHICH HOUSE TEMPORARY EXHIBITIONS, A RESEARCH CENTER, AND OFFICES, LOOK INTO THE HALLS OF THE NAVIGATION MUSEUM.

THE SPATIAL EXPERIENCE IS MODULATED BY THE CONTRAST
BETWEEN TUNNEL-LIKE CONTAINER INTERIORS AND THE EXPANSIVE
HALLS DEFINED BY WALLS OF STACKED CONTAINERS.

THE ALTERNATING RHYTHM OF NARROW ENCLOSURES AND
SUDDEN, WIDE OPENINGS LINKS SPATIAL AND EMOTIONAL
EXPERIENCES, SUGGESTING THE SURPRISE OF DISCOVERY
AND THE EXCITEMENT OF EXPLORATION.

EXTRANEOUS FILL IMMERGE INCORPORATE INCUBATE INFEST INFILTRATE INJECT INSERT

GUZMAN PENTHOUSE
RESIDENCE
NEW YORK 1996

A MECHANICAL SPACE IS TRANSFORMED INTO A LIVING AREA
WITH A SMALL BEDROOM ADDED ABOVE TO CREATE A ROOFTOP
RESIDENCE SITUATED JUST BELOW THE EMPIRE STATE BUILDING.

A BAY WINDOW AT THE MAIN LEVEL AND THE UPSTAIRS BEDROOM
ARE STACKED ON TOP OF EACH OTHER LIKE MODULAR STRUCTURES.

BEDROOM

PATIO

BAY WINDOW

BEDROOM

PATIO

BEDROOM

PATIO

BAY WINDOW

READ

WATCH

LISTEN

LOOK

THE BAY WINDOW—THE BACK PORTION OF A TRUCK CONTAINER—
IS WEDGED INTO THE SOUTH WALL, WHILE THE MASTER BEDROOM,
A 20-FOOT-LONG TRUCK CONTAINER, IS PERCHED ON TOP OF THE
EXISTING STRUCTURE.

THE YELLOW ALUMINUM CONTAINER IS PARTIALLY PEELED OF
ITS WALLS TO CREATE AN OUTDOOR PATIO.

IN THE MINIMAL INTERIOR, EFFICIENTLY INSULATED AND AIR
CONDITIONED, A BED ON TRACKS MOVES IN AND OUT OF A CLOSET
TO ALLOW SLEEPING AS WELL AS LOUNGING.

AN INTERNAL STEEL FIRE-ESCAPE LADDER CONNECTS THE BEDROOM TO THE LIVING ROOM. THE INTERIOR OF THE EXISTING STRUCTURE IS RETURNED TO A SIMPLE WHITE SHELL WITH EXPOSED STEEL PIPES AND BEAMS.

IT HOUSES AN OPEN LAYOUT OF LIVING / DINING / KITCHEN, AND A SEPARATE BEDROOM FOR A CHILD. THE LONGITUDINAL WALL CONSTITUTES THE VISUAL AND FUNCTIONAL SPINE OF THIS LOFT SPACE.

REFRIGERATORS AND NEWSPAPER DISPENSERS PIERCE THIS WALL AND STRETCH THE INTERIOR SPACE TOWARD THE OUTSIDE. NEWSPAPER DISPENSERS BECOME SMALL WINDOWS AND THE ONLY LOOKOUT POINTS ALONG THE WALL.

AN EXPOSED GRID OF BOLTS COMPRESSES AN INSULATION LAYER BETWEEN A CORRUGATED METAL SKIN ON THE OUTSIDE AND THE EXISTING WALL.

THE INTERIOR SIDE OF THE WALL IS LEFT UNFINISHED BUT FLUSH, AND THE TRACED CONSTRUCTION GUIDELINES REMAIN VISIBLE.

THE REFRIGERATOR BOXES ARE GIVEN TECHNOLOGICAL FUNCTIONS: *LISTEN* (HI-FI SYSTEM); *WATCH* (INTERCOM, PULL-OUT TV SET AND MONITOR CONNECTED TO A SURVEILLANCE CAMERA TRAINED TO THE EMPIRE STATE BUILDING); *READ* (BOOKCASE).

INTERCEPT INTERFERE INTERSECT INTRUDE INVADE JUT MERGE NIDIFICATION OCCUPY OVERLAP PARASITE PENETRATE PERTURB

PERFORATE PERMEATE PIERCE PROSTHESIS PROTRUDE PROTUBERANCE

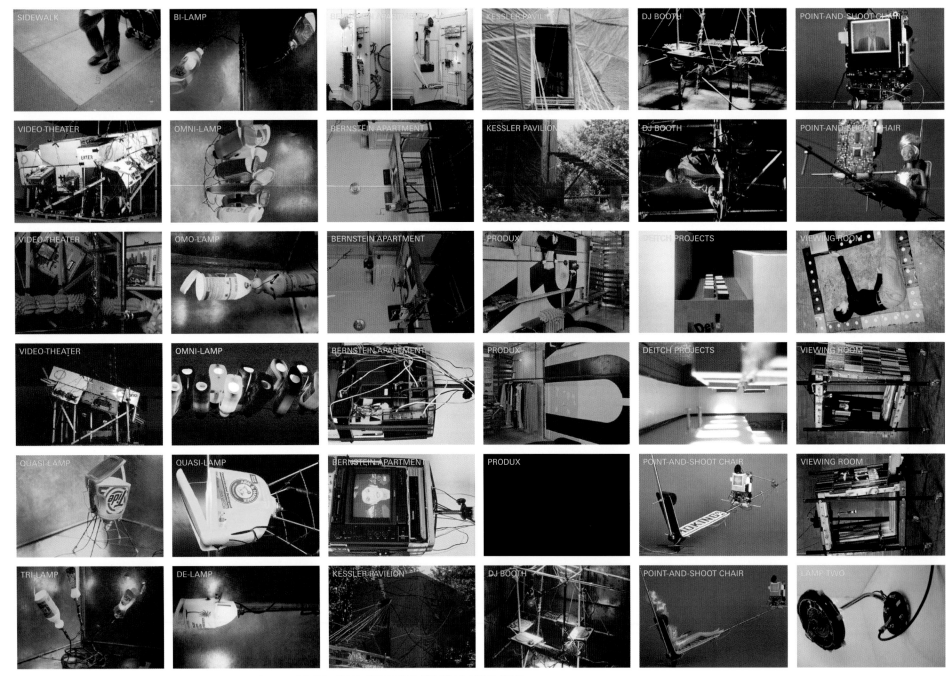

SATURATE STRATIFY SUNK SWALLOW TENTACULAR VIRUS WRAP

INSPIRO-TAINER
COMMISSION FOR THE EXHIBITION *WORKSPHERES*
MUSEUM OF MODERN ART
NEW YORK 2001

AN AIRPLANE CARGO CONTAINER IS TRANSFORMED INTO AN
INDIVIDUAL WORKSTATION IN WHICH THE BOUNDARIES BETWEEN
WORK / PLAY, ACTIVITY / RELAXATION, ISOLATION / COMMUN-
ICATION, AND MEDITATION / ENTERTAINMENT, ARE BLURRED.

THE CONTAINER IS CONCEIVED AS A MODULAR UNIT THAT CAN PROVIDE COMPLETE ISOLATION OR BE COMBINED TO ALLOW TEAMWORK. ITS TOP / FRONT PORTION OPENS UP TO CONNECT TO MORE INSPIRO-TAINERS AND TO CREATE A MEETING ROOM.

INSIDE, THE CONTAINER IS FITTED WITH A MOVABLE SEAT AND DESK THAT ALLOW THE USER'S BODY TO GO FROM A RECLINING TO AN UPRIGHT POSITION.

BOTH SEAT AND TOP ARE OPERATED BY HYDRAULIC PISTONS CONNECTED TO TWO SEPARATE PUMPS INSTALLED ON THE BACK OF THE CONTAINER.

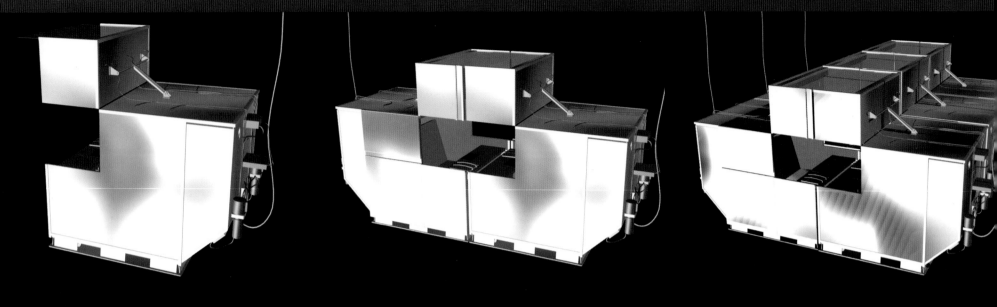

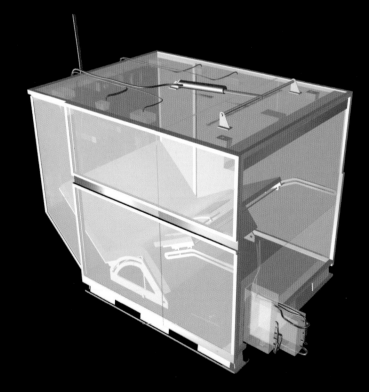

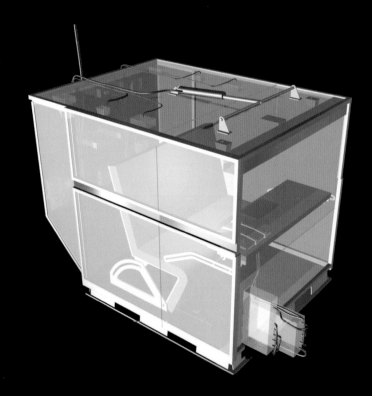

ALL INSIDE SURFACES ARE LINED WITH CONVOLUTED
FOAM USED BOTH AS PADDING AND ACOUSTIC INSULATION.

THE INSPIRO-TAINER IS AN INCUBATOR FOR IDEAS. IT IS EQUIPPED
WITH COMPUTER, FLAT-SCREEN MONITOR, DVD / CD PLAYER,
SURROUND-SOUND SPEAKERS, LCD PROJECTOR AND RETRACT-
ABLE SCREEN, READING LIGHTS, AND VENTILATION FANS.

THE USER CAN EASILY SELECT AND ACTIVATE ALL TECHNOLOGIES
AND MECHANISMS THROUGH A TOUCH-SCREEN PANEL.

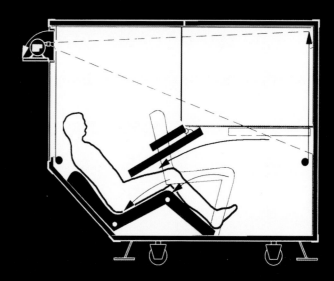

ABSTRACT ABSTRACTION APPARITION ASSUMPTION

BRAIN CEREBRAL CODE CONCEPT CONCEPTUAL CONCEPTUALIZE CONCOCT CORE DREAM ESSENCE ESSENTIAL FANTASY FORMULA GEOMETRY HALLUCINATION HYPOTHETICAL IDEA IDEAL

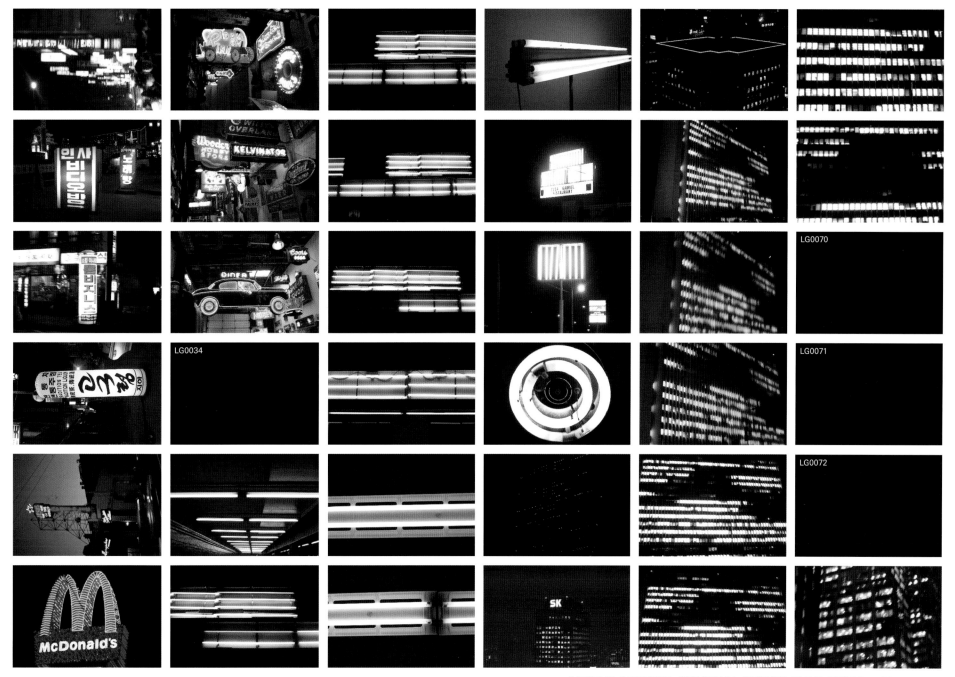

IMAGINARY IMPRACTICAL INTELLECTUAL INTENTION INVENT INVENTION LOGICAL

AN ILLUMINATION AND SURVEILLANCE DEVICE MARKS THE
NARROW CORRIDOR CONNECTING TWO PREVIOUSLY SEPARATE
APARTMENTS.

IT RECREATES THE EXPERIENCE OF PASSING THROUGH A METAL
DETECTOR, AND ACTS AS A LUMINOUS BUFFER BETWEEN THE
OUTSIDE WORLD AND THE PRIVACY OF A HOME.

FOUR CLEAR RESIN PANELS ARE STACKED AND ATTACHED TO THE CORRIDOR'S WALLS, TWO ON EITHER SIDE. THE PANELS ARE CAST USING A PLASTIC SHIPPING PALLET AS THE MOLD.

SIX NEON TUBES AND ONE SURVEILLANCE CAMERA ARE EMBEDDED IN THE CAST OF EACH PANEL. TOGETHER, THEY ILLUMINATE AND SURVEY THE PASSAGE OF PEOPLE THROUGH THE CORRIDOR AS THEY ENTER THE APARTMENT.

IMAGES FROM THE CAMERAS ARE DISPLAYED ON FOUR FLAT-SCREEN MONITORS AFFIXED TO THE LIVING ROOM WALL. THE BODY PASSING THROUGH THE CORRIDOR IS BROKEN UP AND RECOMPOSED IN FOUR VIEWS.

MENTAL METAPHOR RATIONAL SCHEME SYMBOLIC THEORY THEORETICAL THOUGHT TRANSCENDENT TYPE TYPICAL UNAPPLIED VISION VISIONARY VISUAL VISUALIZE

ACCELERATE BYPASS CINEMATIC CIRCULATE

A STEEL PIPE STRUCTURE RESTS ON THE FLOOR OF THE MAIN GALLERY. IT CONTAINS A LONG VOLUME DIVIDED INTO NINE PROJECTION ROOMS.

THE STEEL STRUCTURE ALSO HOLDS THREE PROJECTORS THAT THROW LARGE IMAGES ON THE OPPOSITE WALL. AN INTENSE BLUE ATMOSPHERE ENVELOPS THE WHOLE SPACE.

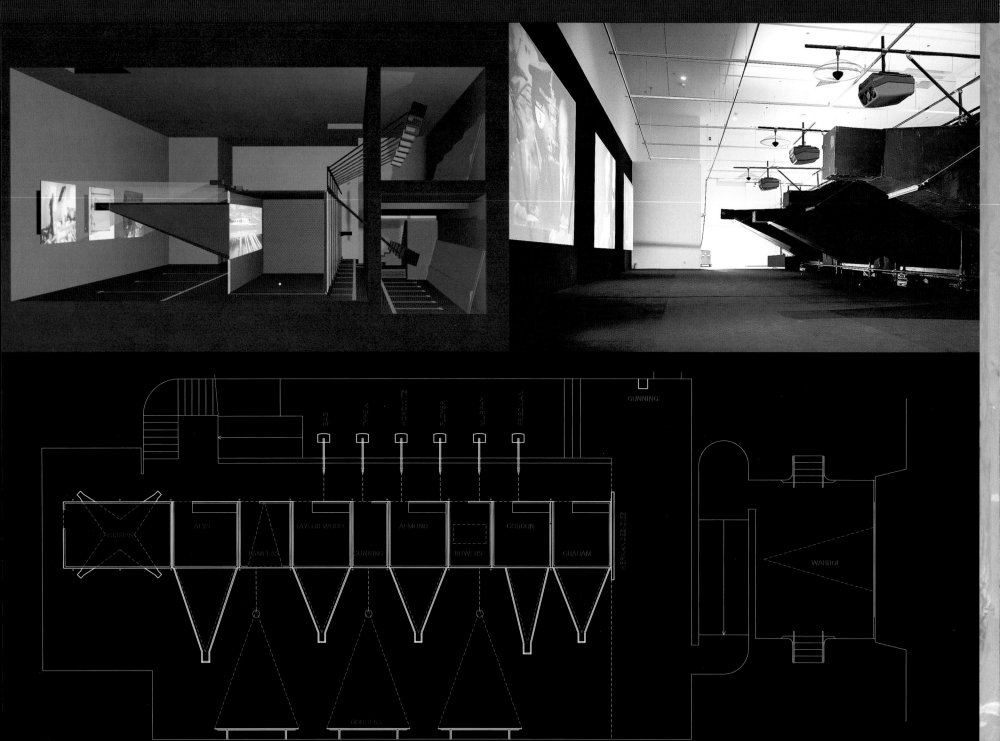

EACH ROOM IS AN INDIVIDUAL PROJECTION BOOTH SCALED ACCORDING TO EACH SPECIFIC PROJECTION SIZE AND FITTED WITH A BENCH AND LINED ENTIRELY WITH ACOUSTIC FOAM.

THE IMAGES ARE REAR PROJECTED ONTO THE SCREENS TO ELIMINATE ANY INTERFERENCE BETWEEN THE PROJECTIONS AND THE VIEWERS' BODIES.

BLACK CONES ENVELOP THE PROJECTORS AND THEIR CONES OF LIGHT, PROTRUDING FROM ONE SIDE OF THE MAIN VOLUME.

ON THE OPPOSITE SIDE, THE STEEL STRUCTURE PENETRATES THE MUSEUM WALL TO HOLD MONITORS IN BOTH LOWER AND UPPER SIDE GALLERIES.

A SLANTED WALL, LINED WITH BLUE VINYL COATED FOAM, IS POSITIONED OPPOSITE TO THE LINES OF MONITORS TO ALLOW VIEWERS TO LEAN AND WATCH VIDEOS.

MT0012

COMMUTE DRIVE-IN DRIVE-THRU DROP-OFF DYNAMIC

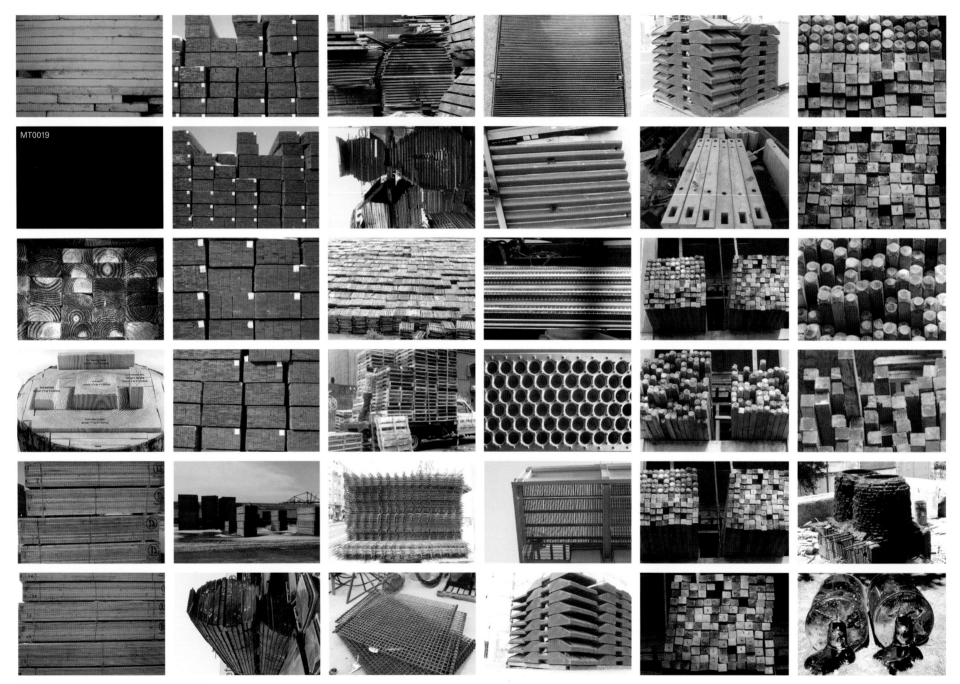

MT0019

EMIGRATE ERRANT ERRATIC EXPRESS FAST

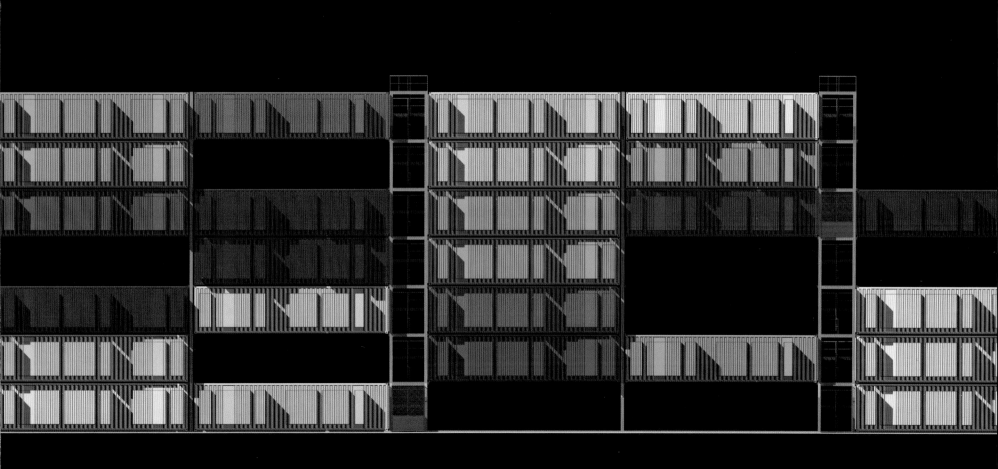

ONCE IT REACHES ITS DESTINATION, THE MDU IS LOADED ONTO A VERTICAL MDU HARBOR, TO BE FOUND IN ALL MAJOR METROPOLITAN AREAS AROUND THE GLOBE.

THE HARBOR IS A MULTIPLE LEVEL STEEL RACK, MEASURING 8 FEET IN WIDTH (THE WIDTH OF ONE CONTAINER) AND VARYING IN LENGTH ACCORDING TO THE SITE.

ITS LINEAR DEVELOPMENT PROFILE IS GENERATED BY THE REPETITION OF MDUS AND VERTICAL DISTRIBUTION CORRIDORS. ELEVATORS, STAIRS, AND ALL SERVICE FACILITIES (POWER, DATA, WATER, SEWAGE) RUN VERTICALLY ALONG THESE CORRIDORS.

A CRANE SLIDES PARALLEL, ALONG THE ENTIRE LENGTH OF THE BUILDING, ON ITS OWN TRACK. THE CRANE PICKS UP MDUS AS THEY ARE DRIVEN TO THE SITE AND LOADS THEM ONTO SLOTS ALONG THE RACK.

STEEL BRACKETS SUPPORT AND SECURE MDUS IN THEIR ASSIGNED POSITIONS, WHERE THEY ARE PLUGGED INTO ALL SERVICE SYSTEMS.

THE VERTICAL HARBOR IS IN CONSTANT TRANSFORMATION AS MDUS ARE LOADED AND UNLOADED FROM THE PERMANENT RACK.

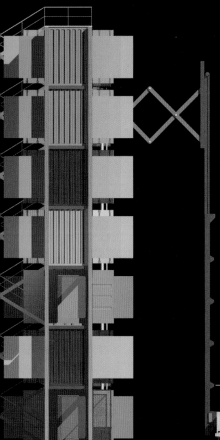
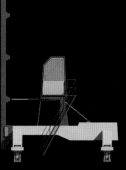

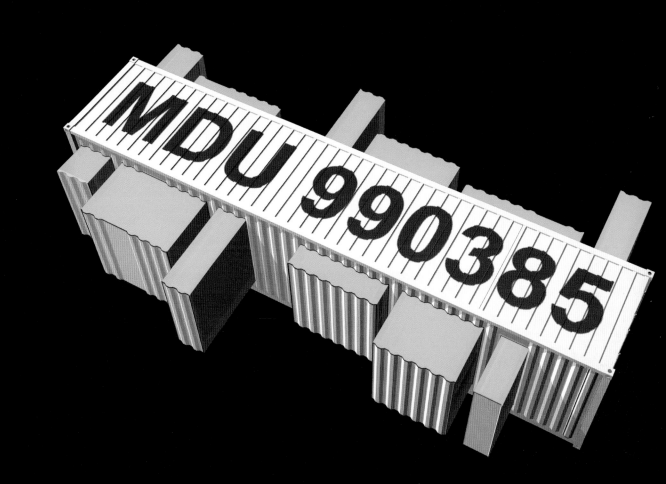

CUTS IN THE METAL WALLS OF THE CONTAINER GENERATE EXTRUDED SUBVOLUMES, EACH HOUSING A LIVE, WORK, OR STORAGE FUNCTION.

WHEN TRAVELING, THESE SUBVOLUMES ARE PUSHED INTO THE CONTAINER, INTERLOCKING WITH EACH OTHER AND LEAVING THE OUTER SKIN FLUSH TO ALLOW FOR SHIPPING.

WHEN IN USE, ALL SUBVOLUMES ARE PUSHED OUT, LEAVING THE INTERIOR OF THE CONTAINER COMPLETELY UNOBSTRUCTED WITH ALL FUNCTIONS ACCESSIBLE ALONG ITS SIDES.

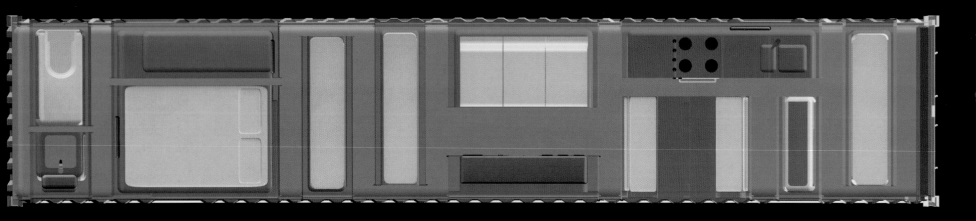

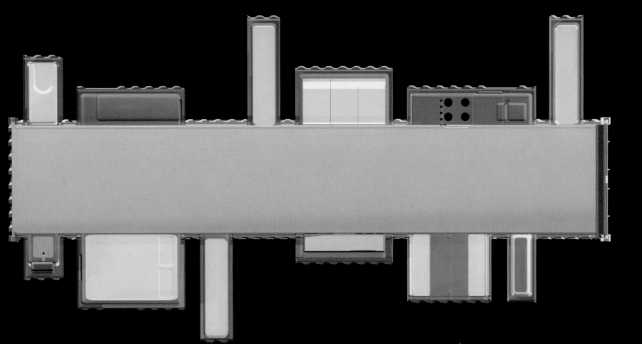

THE INTERIOR OF THE CONTAINER AND THE SUBVOLUMES ARE FABRICATED ENTIRELY OUT OF FIBERGLASS, INCLUDING ALL BUILT-IN FIXTURES AND FURNISHINGS.

A CENTRAL COMPUTER REGULATES AIRFLOW AND TEMPERATURE AS WELL AS LIGHTING; IT IS CONNECTED TO EXTERNAL COMMUNICATION NETWORKS AND TO MONITORS, SPEAKERS, AND MICROPHONES DISTRIBUTED THROUGHOUT THE UNIT.

MILLER-JONES STUDIO
LIVE / WORK LOFT
NEW YORK 1996

THE SIDE OF A 40-FOOT-LONG ALUMINUM SHIPPING CONTAINER CUTS ACROSS A WAREHOUSE SPACE WITH VARIOUS FUNCTIONS ALIGNED ALONG ITS AXIS.

THE TWO-DIMENSIONAL NATURE OF THIS ELEMENT IS EXPLOITED TO DEFINE A SHEAR EDGE BETWEEN PRIVATE AND PROFESSIONAL NEEDS. ONLY TECHNOLOGICAL APPLIANCES EMERGE WHEN IT IS COMPLETELY CLOSED.

BATHROOM

KITCHEN

BEDROOM

LIVING / STUDIO

mobile work station

multi-functional wo

A SYSTEM OF INCISIONS BREAKS THE CONTAINER INTO
A MECHANISM OF ROTATING PANELS THAT, WHEN OPENED,
RE-ESTABLISH THE CONTINUITY OF THE SPACES REVEALED
BEHIND THEM: BEDROOM, KITCHEN, AND STORAGE SPACES.

THE SIDE OF THE CONTAINER ALSO PENETRATES THE BATHROOM
TO BECOME A SHOWER PARTITION.

FLOATING ON CASTERS IN THE MAIN SPACE, AN ISLAND MADE OUT OF FOUR REFRIGERATORS CONTAINS ALL WORK FUNCTIONS. THE REFRIGERATORS SERVE AS STORAGE WHILE THEIR DOORS SERVE AS ADDITIONAL WORK SURFACES WHEN LIFTED OPEN.

A WOOD TOP ON TRACKS IS PARTED DOWN THE MIDDLE AND PULLS OUT TO CREATE TWO DESKS AT OPPOSITE ENDS OF THE ISLAND. ONE END IS EQUIPPED WITH A DRAFTING BOARD THAT SLIDES ON ITS OWN TRACKS; A COMPUTER IS IMBEDDED AT THE OTHER END.

THE SCANNER AND PRINTER SLIDE OUT OF THE FORMER FREEZER COMPARTMENT. BOTH ENDS ARE FURNISHED WITH A PULLOUT LAMP AND ELECTRIC OUTLETS.

FLASH HECTIC HOMELESSNESS IMMIGRANT JAMMED JUMP KINETIC MANEUVER MOBILE MOBILITY

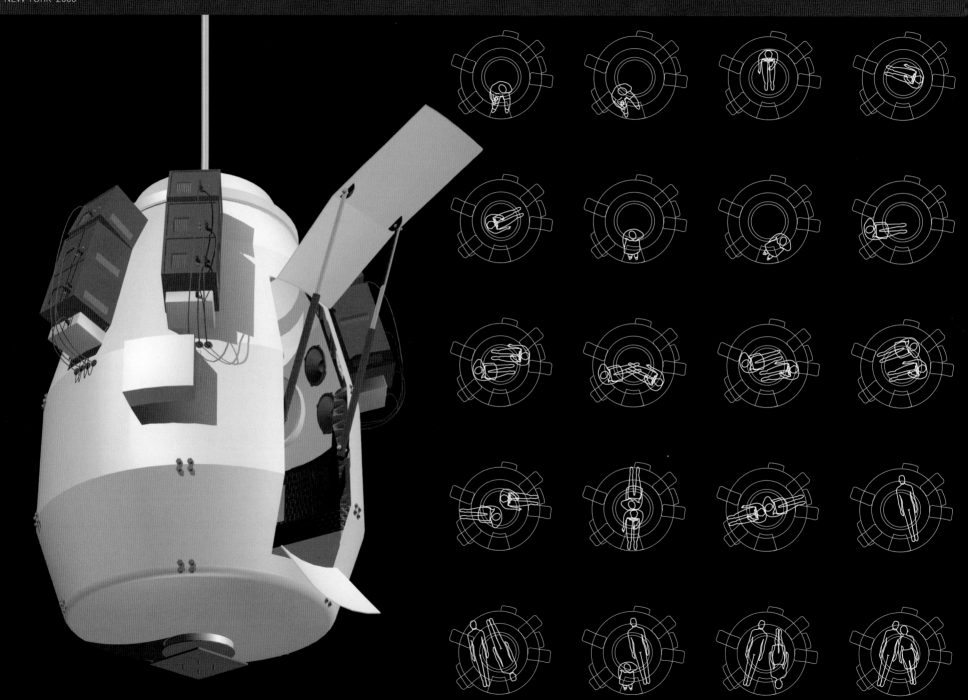

MIXER
MEDIA COCOON,
HENRY URBACH ARCHITECTURE GALLERY
NEW YORK 2000

A STEEL CEMENT MIXER IS TRANSFORMED INTO A TWENTY-FIRST-
CENTURY MEDIA COCOON SUITABLE FOR LOUNGING, VIEWING,
AND DREAMING.

FITTED WITH VERTICAL BANKS OF 12-INCH MONITORS CONNECTED TO A VARIETY OF AUDIO / VIDEO INPUTS, MIXER OFFERS A PLUSH, INTIMATE ENVIRONMENT ANIMATED BY MULTIPLE FORMS OF INFORMATION, ENTERTAINMENT, AND MEDIA.

AS MIXER PIVOTS ON ITS CENTRAL AXIS, SURVEILLANCE CAMERA 1 SURVEYS THE ROOM IN WHICH THE MIXER IS LOCATED.

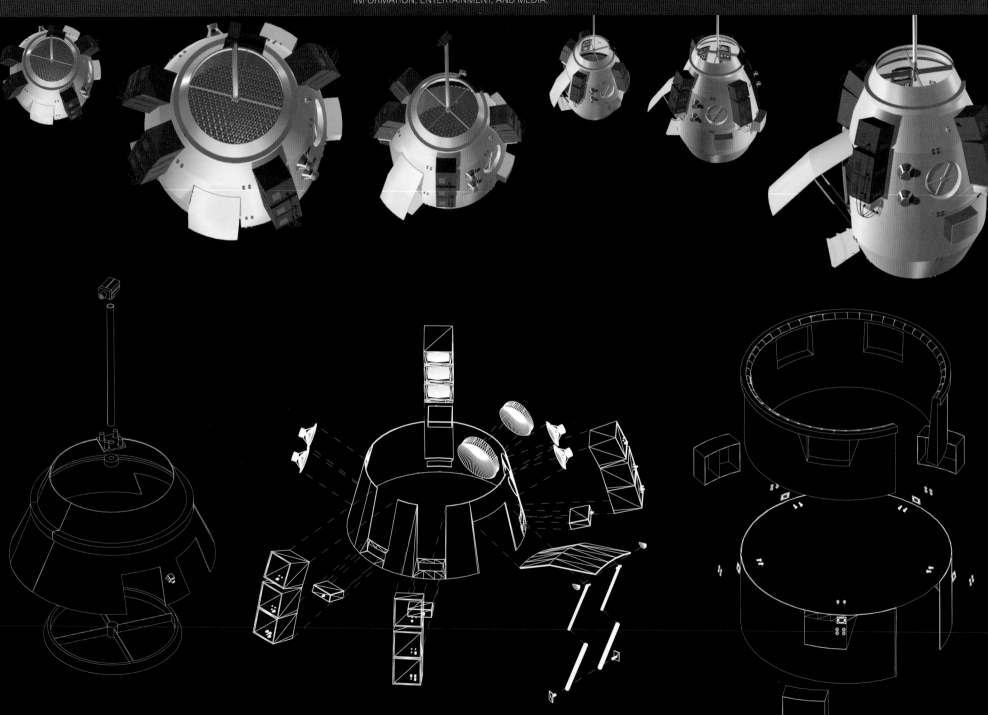

CABLES EXTENDING FROM THE UPPER SLIP RING REACH THE ROOF OF THE BUILDING TO CONNECT TO SATELLITE TV AND TO SURVEILLANCE CAMERA 2.

CITY LANDSCAPES ARE TRANSMITTED TO THE MONITORS INSIDE THE MIXER TOGETHER WITH THE INFINITE CHANNEL SELECTION OF SATELLITE TV.

PLAYSTATION 2 BRINGS VIRTUAL REALITY GAMES, MOVIES, AND FAST INTERNET CONNECTIVITY INTO THE CAPSULE.

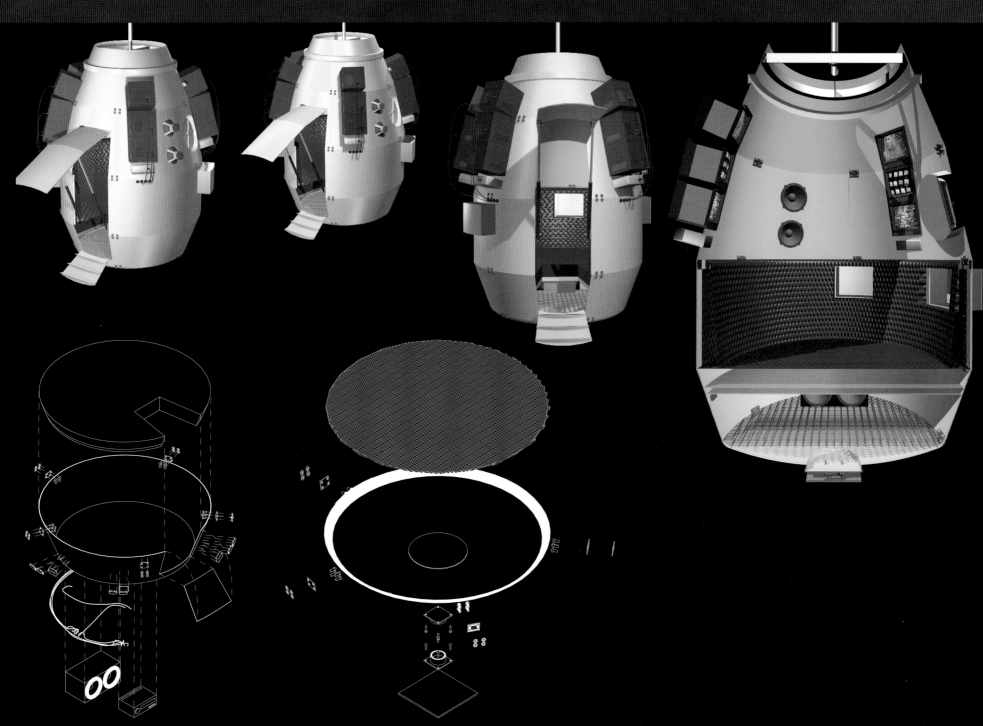

RESTING ON THE EXTRA-SOFT BLUE FOAM, USERS CAN CREATE MULTIPLE VISUAL CONFIGURATIONS ON THE TWELVE SCREENS THROUGH A CENTRAL ROUTER.

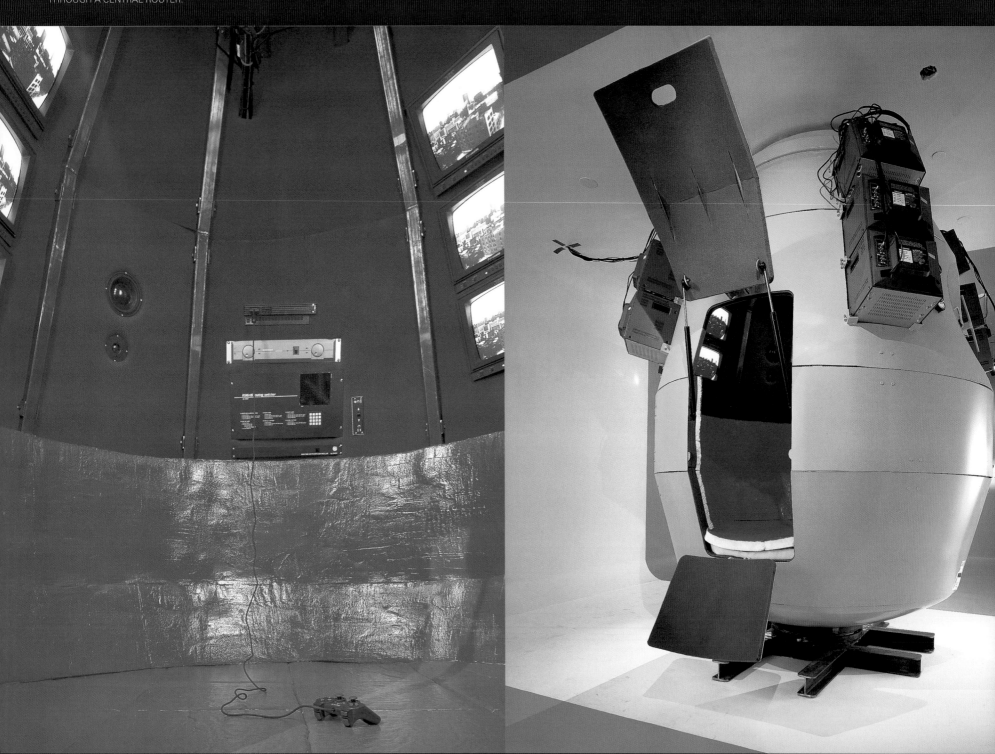

MIXER OFFERS, IN THE SPIRIT OF A DJ MIXING BOOTH, A SPACE
TO SELECT, SAMPLE, AND MIX SOUND AND IMAGERY TO SUIT
INDIVIDUAL FANTASIES.

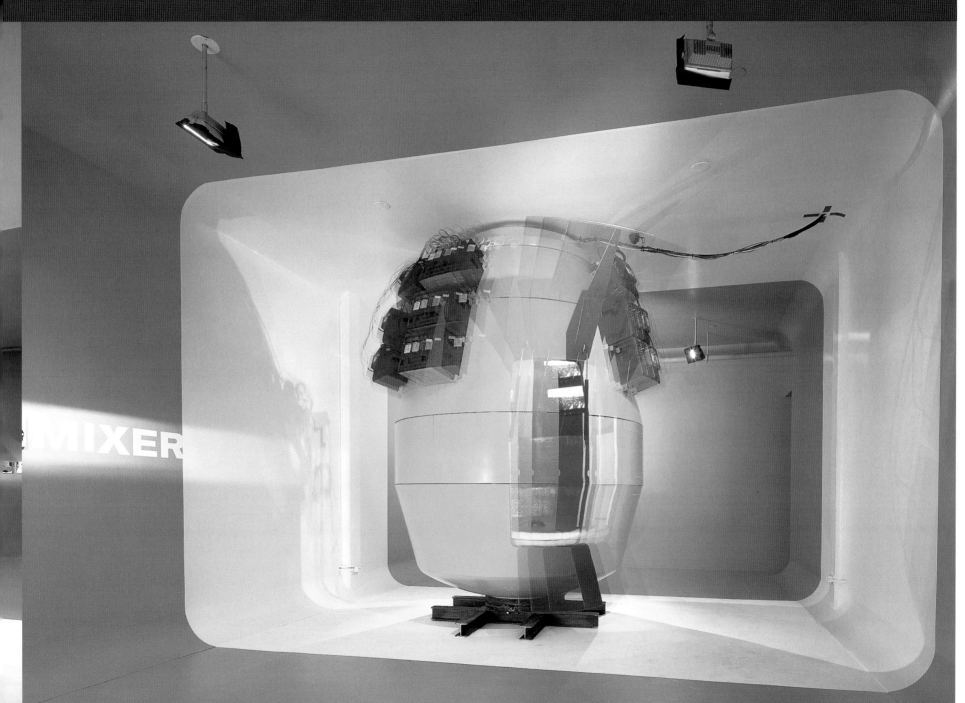

Notes on the lessons of technology in William Gibson / Philip Nobel

> Not the least of William Gibson's accomplishments was to foresee, beginning in 1984 with his cyberpunk classic *Neuromancer*, that the highest and lowest technologies are never mutually exclusive; in any but the most rigid economic and political contexts, they are inseparable. That novel, in which a software pirate sets out into the matrix and encounters the birth of a global artificial intelligence, may be best known as a vehicle for Gibson's coinage "cyberspace." It is also remarkable for the attention it gives to resistant technologies at the other end of the complexity spectrum. Away from his sentient, prescient Web, we see old copper wires and cardboard walls, broken glass, duct tape, and blunt shivs. Sometimes the high exists within the shell of the low, the low sometimes trumps the high, but what we get is a projection of a world where all technologies thrive, each in its niche, each doing what only it can do. Which is why it feels so real.

> There have long been fictional intimations of the clash and balance of Gibson's all-tech ecosystem. Throughout the canon, whether in Frank Herbert's protracted medieval-future *Dune* series or in the deliberately contrasting accouterments of *Star Wars*—sand and silicon—we find that the most believable futures leave no techniques behind. But all of these relatively recent meditations on technological heterogeneity—among which *Blade Runner* is still the most complete—represent a sweeping revision of an older school, whole futurescapes where monolithic technologies were a given: The pure worlds of Isaac Asimov and Arthur C. Clarke and their precursors in film, going back to *Aelita, Queen of Mars*; the singular tool-of-tools that enlightened and then destroyed the hapless Krell on that *Forbidden Planet*, Altair-IV. Such forecasts are always set in an authoritarian context, whether explicit, as in *Logan's Run*, with its namesake dash to freedom in the ruins of Washington, D.C., or implied, as in *Star Trek*. A pure future is a fascist future, as we all know, looking at Germany, looking at France. Only through central control do the grandest architecture and the most sublimely uniform streetscapes arise. In a democracy, new technologies don't expunge the old, they just push their rivals aside to serve the needs of other, more marginal economies. There, the old may linger, flourish, or spawn the unknowing devotions of a thousand cargo cults, but it does not die.

> That churning of tools and techniques through culture and class, where a cast-off machine can coincide—or interface—with the crystalline Net, is what William Gibson celebrates. As a result, an intensely democratic feel suffuses his septet of near-future novels. Several of which,

like the most recent, *All Tomorrow's Parties*, are staged on an earthquake damaged and re-colonized San Francisco-Oakland Bay Bridge. Until it is destroyed by a multinational trying to recapture its intellectual property—that ultimate hybrid of old and new, the physical fax machine—the bridge is a violent but communal Petri dish for a laissez-faire technological ecology, coming soon to a world near you. Fiberglass to carbon fiber to fiber optics: low tech keeps the rain out, but high tech makes the culture move.

> The problem of how a more determined architecture (versus the shanty-town trope of Gibson's freetown) can navigate this technological evolution is sometimes cast as one of the most pressing issues facing the practice today. During the very early 1990s, when the promise of virtual reality technology flowered briefly before romance and investment capital migrated to the Internet, a little-known New York group calling itself "Arcathexis" took this problem as its own. Which way would architects go? Would they stay on the margins, keeping out the rain? Or would they claim a role in technology, going into the wires to build-out the sprawl of the public-domain matrix that then seemed so imminent? An unpublished but privately-circulated "protomanifesto" written by the group in 1991 sought to argue for that second path: "This is an exciting time in architecture, and a strange time to herald its death," the anonymous authors wrote in the resounding and turgid style that is their signature:

At this one hysterical moment, architects are concerned with preserving relics of history, and, through postmodern buildings, resurrecting the mute classical language, while others flirt with sci-fi hi-tech [sic] or idly attempt to deconstruct the very notion of architecture itself. Never before have such a disparate lot of dissipated styles and venal urges coexisted...and one would think, as many do, that this fervor springs from fecund ground. These observers see opportunity where we see OBSOLESCENCE. We are witnessing the death throes of architecture as a built art, and, like an arrow at the end of its arc, it wavers, indicating many targets.

Of the foreseeable future states of architecture, they wrote, many are dim. If the profession continues on its present course, further divorcing itself from the art of building while pursuing a regimen of "neutered introspection," masking "self-aggrandizing (ultimately suicidal) myth-making," there will remain nothing in architecture "but the banter of a cabal of BUFFOONS and some very thin facades." Writing in a mode that seems to prefigure the rhetoric of the Internet enthusiasts who would arrive a few years later, they saw salvation in "a nascent technology that promises to create an infinite realm of VIRGIN SPACE."

> As Frank Lloyd Wright did in his 1901 lecture "The Art and Craft of the Machine," Arcathexis argued that the chance to create a vital architectural language had not existed since the Middle Ages. Then, they suggest, the architect was the able recorder of a societal worldview, and thus the preeminent shaper of its self-image, "lasting and ephemeral." Like Wright, too, they hang their argument on "Ceci Tuera Cela," a chapter of Victor Hugo's Notre-Dame de Paris that is often omitted from English translations. Hugo argued, in roundabout terms that give one sympathy for the editors' omission, that the invention of the printing press forever dethroned architecture as a location for cultural-currency, leaving it petrified in a world of more facile exchange; the "words" in stone could not compete— in power or permanence—with those on paper; a new communications technology had elbowed aside the old. Since that revolution, they contended, "architecture has labored to re-establish itself in the domain of the printed word." But despite "the achievements of [contemporary] architecture" in making buildings "speak," to Arcathexis, each of its heroes is ultimately a tragic figure, "for such dreams were and are impossible to realize in a society in possession of a vastly more fluid form of communication." Of course, given that this was a manifesto, it ended on a progressive note:

The coming TECHNOLOGICAL REVOLUTION holds the key to a true ARCHITECTURAL RENAISSANCE, if one caveat is accepted: to prosper in the future the institutions and practice of architecture must ABANDON building in favor of VIRTUAL CONSTRUCTION.

In its enthusiasm for overturning architectural shibboleths, the "protomanifesto" argues that architecture will thrive only in an either/or technological landscape: Stone or steel or cyberspace. But it does not have to be either/or—indeed, the fact that we live in a nominal democracy, with a loosely regulated economy, would suggest that pure, sweeping displacement is an unlikely mode for technological development. (If we begin to see otherwise, it would be cause for concern.) The lesson of Gibson—who seems to lurk just beneath the surface of Arcathexis's rampant imaginations—is that, now and forever, technological change is a both/and condition.

> In his 1981 short story "Johnny Mnemonic," Gibson sets this principal to action. The title character, himself a demicyborg at the apogee of technology, carries locked within him the for-hire memories of countless feuding corporations. One company wants them out, and Johnny won't survive the extraction. Pure instrumentality is at the mercy of raw force; for help he turns to an urban tribe called the Lo Teks. It's not the machine in the garden; it's the machine in the junkyard: "The Lo Teks leach their webs and huddling places to

the city's fabric with thick gobs of epoxy and sleep above the abyss in mesh hammocks. Their country is so attenuated that in places it consists of holds for hands and feet, sawed into geodesic struts." As our hybrid hero is led up into refuge in their future-primitive aerie of re-purposed industrial detritus, the copious graffiti on the weathered domes gradually fades until only a single name appears: "LO TEK. In dripping black capitals."

> "Who's Lo Tek?" he asks his guide.

> "Not us, boss."

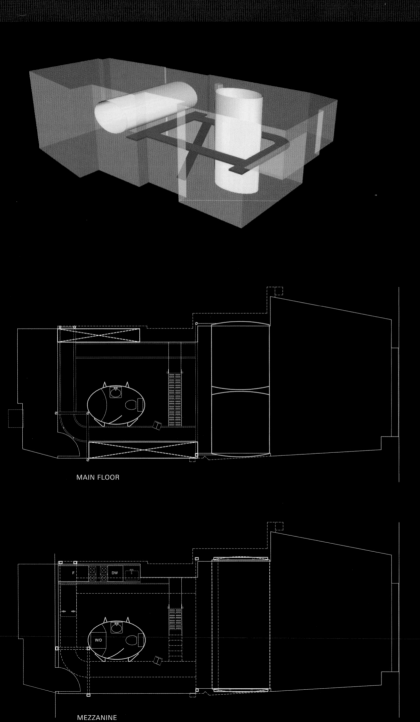

MAIN FLOOR

MEZZANINE

THE TANK IS CUT IN TWO SECTIONS THAT ENCLOSE INTIMATE FUNCTIONS, LEAVING THE SURROUNDING SPACE UNDIVIDED AND UNOBSTRUCTED.

ONE OF THE TWO SECTIONS IS PLACED HORIZONTALLY OVER THE LIVING ROOM AND CONTAINS TWO SLEEPING PODS.

TWO LARGE HATCHBACK DOORS, CUT FROM EACH SIDE OF THE TANK, ARE CONNECTED TO HYDRAULIC PISTONS AND OPEN UP AT THE PUSH OF A BUTTON TO OFFER SUNLIGHT AND VENTILATION TO THOSE IN BED.

A SYSTEM OF METAL-GRATING CATWALKS, FILLED WITH CLEAR RESIN, GIVES ACCESS AT THE MEZZANINE LEVEL TO THE UPPER BATHROOM, THE SLEEPING PODS, AND TO THE CLOSETS ON EITHER SIDE OF THE SPACE.

THE SECOND SECTION IS PLACED VERTICALLY FROM FLOOR TO CEILING. IT CONTAINS TWO BATHROOMS STACKED ONE ON TOP OF THE OTHER.

MOVEMENT MOTION NAVIGATE NOMAD ORBIT OSCILLATE PATH RUSH RHYTHM

SHORTCUT SPIN STIR TAKE-OFF TRAFFIC TRANSIT TRANSPORT TRAJECTORY VAGRANT VECTOR VEHICLE VELOCITY WANDER

PK0034

ACCESS AIRLINE AIRMAIL ANTENNA AUDIO BROADCAST CABLE

CELL PHONE   CHANNEL   COMMUNICATE   CONNECTION   DIALTONE

E-MAIL ENTER EXIT FREQUENCY GLOBALIZATION HUB INTERFACE KEYBOARD KEYPAD LINK MESH MONITOR MULTICHANNEL MULTIDIMENSIONAL

MULTIDIRECTIONAL MULTIMEDIA NET NETWORK NODE ONLINE ON-SCREEN RADAR SATELLITE SIGNAL

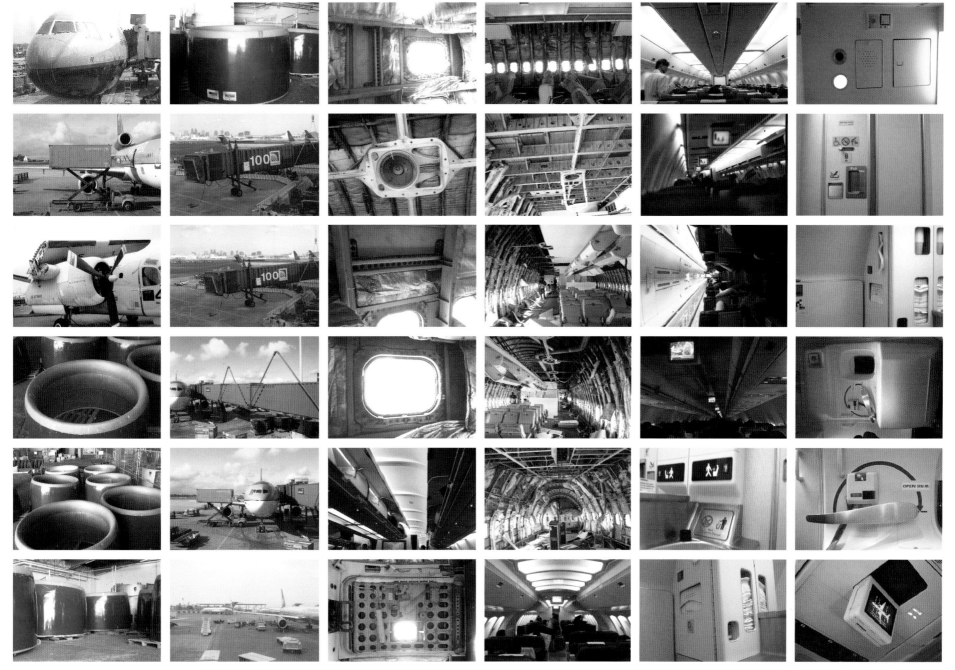

SIMULCAST SURVEILLANCE TECHNOLOGY TELECOMMUNICATION TERMINAL TOUCH TONE TRANSMISSION TRANSMIT VIDEO CONFERENCING

PS0009

WAVELENGTH WEB WIRE WIRED WIRELESS WORLDWIDE

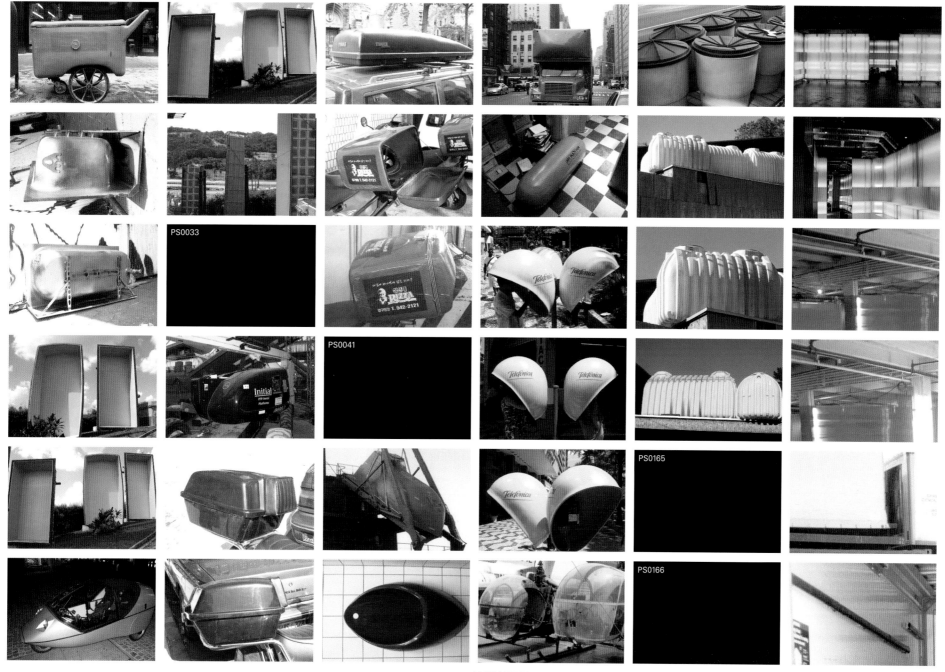

PS0033

PS0041

PS0165

PS0166

ACCESSORIZED AIR-CONDITIONED AIRTIGHT APPLIANCE APPARATUS AUTOMATIC BUILT-IN

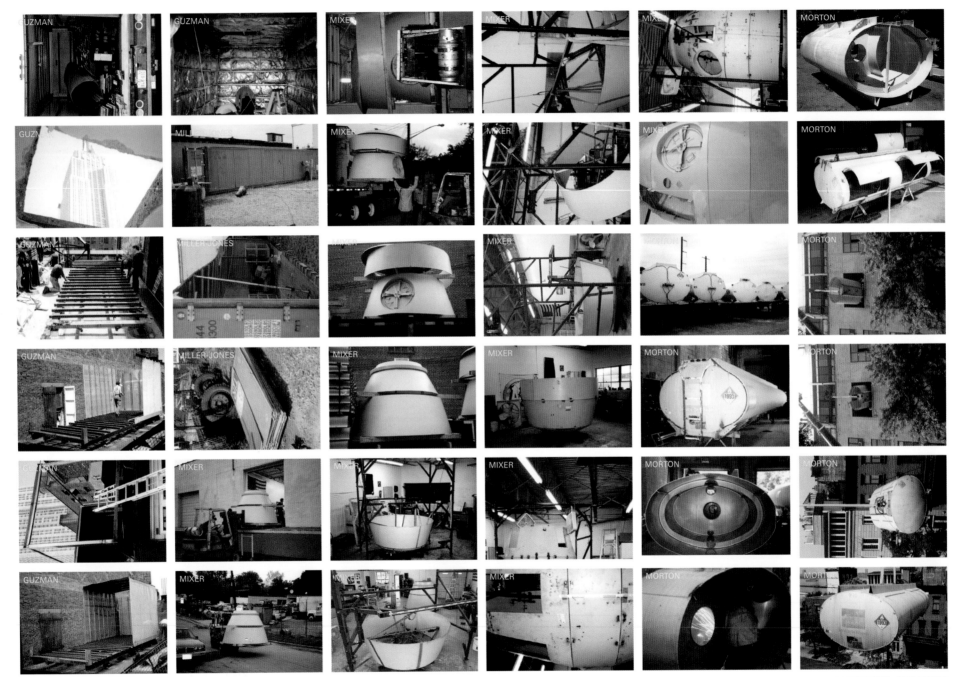

CAPSULE COLLAPSIBLE COMFORTABLE COMPACT COMPARTMENTALIZED CONVENIENT

CONVERTIBLE   CUSTOMIZED   EFFICIENT   ELECTRIC   ELECTRONIC   ENJOY   ERGONOMIC   FUTURISTIC   GADGET   HYDRAULIC   HYGIENIC

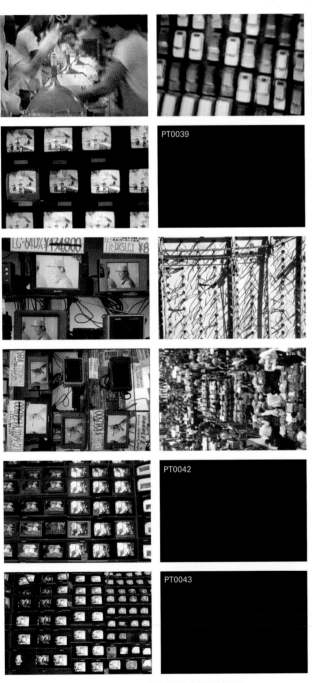

PT0039

PT0042

PT0043

HYPERFUNCTIONAL IMMUNIZED INSULATED MECHANICAL

RET.INEVITABLE 1.5
PROJECTION ROOM
CHICAGO ART FAIR
CHICAGO 1999

RET.INEVITABLE1.5 INVESTIGATES THE EXPERIENCE OF TOTAL ABSORPTION IN A CINEMATOGRAPHIC SPACE. A DYNAMIC ILLUMINATED CORE IS DEFINED WITHIN A LARGE, NONDESCRIPT CONFERENCE ROOM.

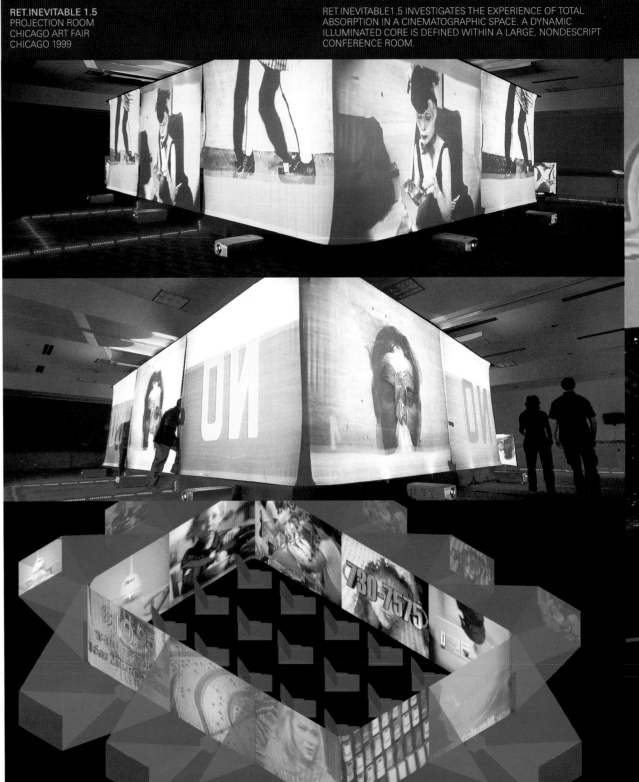

THE VISUAL PROGRAMS ARE REAR PROJECTED ONTO THE CORE WALLS THROUGH LARGE MIRRORS THAT DOUBLE THE SIZE OF THE PROJECTED IMAGES.

RED NAVIGATION LIGHTS DIRECT PEOPLE TO THE ENTRANCE OF THE CORE, WHERE FOUR SLITS BETWEEN THE PROJECTED IMAGES ALLOW ENTRY. ONCE INSIDE, VIDEO, ART AND SHORT FILMS ENGULF VISITORS IN A 360-DEGREE EXPERIENCE.

BLUE, VINYL-COATED LOUNGE CHAIRS ARE MOUNTED ON A TURNTABLE MECHANISM THAT ALLOWS VIEWERS TO SPIN. EACH CHAIR IS EQUIPPED WITH A REMOTE HEADSET SO THAT THE PROGRAM CAN BE TAILORED TO THE VISITOR'S DESIRE.

SARA MELTZER GALLERY
ART GALLERY
NEW YORK 2000

A 10-FOOT-HIGH CONTINUOUS WHITE BAND FOLDS AROUND A FORMER PARKING GARAGE AND IS CANTILEVERED FROM THE PERIMETER WALLS SO THAT IT FLOATS IN SPACE WITHOUT TOUCHING FLOOR OR CEILING.

IT OVERLAPS THE RAW TEXTURE OF THE EXISTING GARAGE WALLS WITH ITS PRISTINE SUPERWHITE SURFACE, CREATING A PURE EXHIBITION LAYER DISTINCT FROM THE STILL-PRESENT PREVIOUS PARKING STRUCTURE.

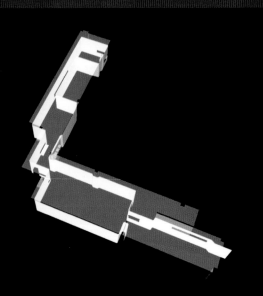

AT THE ENTRANCE, THE BAND ACTS AS THE GALLERY SIGN. ALONG
THE STEEL ENTRY RAMP, THE BAND BECOMES A LIGHT FIXTURE.

AT OTHER POINTS THE BAND'S PATH DETACHES ITSELF FROM THE WALLS TO FOLD OUT AND GENERATE SPACES FOR SERVICE FUNCTIONS (RECEPTION, OFFICES, AND STORAGE).

ALL CORNERS OF THIS NEW SURFACE ARE ROUNDED TO
ENHANCE THE FLOW OF THE WHITE RIBBON THROUGH THE SPACE.
CUTS ALONG ITS SKIN GENERATE WINDOWS BETWEEN SPACES AS
WELL AS FLUORESCENT ILLUMINATED OPENINGS.

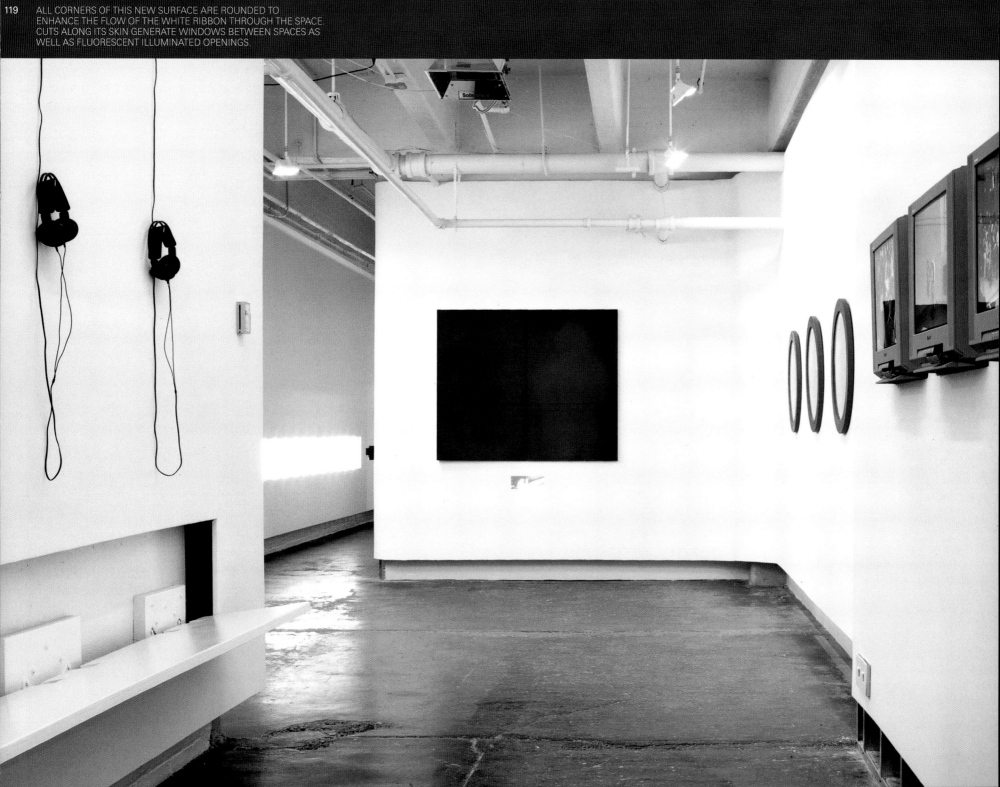

SCRAPS

MICROHABITAT MOTORIZED MOVABLE MULTIFUNCTIONAL MULTIPURPOSE

> 2000
LOT/EK, *MIXER*
(NEW YORK: EDIZIONI PRESS).
DONALD ALBRECHT, ELLEN LUPTON, AND STEVEN SKOV HOLT,
DESIGN CULTURE NOW
(NEW YORK: PRINCETON ARCHITECTURAL PRESS).
> 1999
MATTEO VERCELLONI, *LOFTS AND APARTMENTS IN NYC*
(MILAN: L'ARCHIVOLTO).
CYNTHIA INIONS, *ONE SPACE LIVING*
(LONDON: RYLAND PETERS & SMALL).
MAYER RUS, *LOFT*
(NEW YORK: MONACELLI PRESS).
> 1995
BEVERLY RUSSELL, *40 UNDER 40*
(GRAND RAPIDS, MI: VITAE PUBLISHING).
CARLA BREEZE, *NEW MODERN*
(NEW YORK: P.B.C.).
> 1994
TERENCE CONRAN, *THE ESSENTIAL HOUSE BOOK*
(LONDON: CONRAN OCTOPUS).

> 2001
"LOT/EK ARCHITECTURE: MORTON LOFT," *A+U*.
DANIEL FIERMAN, "PLAYING POD," *I.D.*, APRIL.
MICHELLE HOWRY, "HOME SWEET HOME," *I.D.*, APRIL.
ALBA CAPPELLIERI, "LOT/EK," *DOMUS*, MARCH.
JOHN SEABROOK, "A POD OF ONE'S OWN," THE NEW YORKER,
12 FEBRUARY.
LINDSAY BAKER, "NOBLE SALVAGE," *THE GUARDIAN WEEKEND*,
20 JANUARY.
> 2000
LUCIE YOUNG, "THINK TANK," *NEW YORK TIMES MAGAZINE*,
8 OCTOBER.
MAYER RUS, "THE BUILDING BLOCKS," *W*, OCTOBER.
CHRISTOPHER HAWTHORNE, "THE LOD/OWN ON LOT/EK,"
METROPOLIS, AUGUST/SEPT.
JOSEPH GIOVANNINI, "THE NEW PRIMITIVE HUT," *ARCHITECTURE*,
JANUARY.
> 1999
JAYNE MERKEL, "PRACTICE PROFILE: LOT/EK," *ARCHITECTURAL
DESIGN*, DECEMBER.
P. GIACOPPO, "LOT/EKARCHITECTURE," *DOMUS*, MAY.
JULIE IOVINE, "ARCHITECTURE FOR A NEW CENTURY," *NEW YORK
TIMES*, 11 MARCH.
DEGEN PENER, "TUNNEL VISION," *WALLPAPER*, MARCH.
LISA MATTHEWS, "INDUSTRIALE," *D DI REPUBBLICA*, 23 FEBRUARY.
VICTORIA O'BRIAN, "TRAILER TRASH," *SUNDAY TIMES*, 14 FEBRUARY.
> 1998
ANTHONY IANNACCI, "THINK TANK" *INTERIOR DESIGN*, DECEMBER.
AMY STAFFORD, "LOT/EK," *SURFACE*, JULY.
JESSIE SCANLON "DINETTE SET," *WIRED*, JUNE.
> 1997
RANDY KENNEDY, "LIFE ON THE CARVING EDGE," *NEW YORK TIMES*,
2 OCTOBER.
HENRY URBACH, "POST-INDUSTRIAL STRENGTH," *INTERIOR DESIGN*,
SEPTEMBER.
"ATICO EN NUEVA YORK," DISEÑO INTERIOR, OCTOBER.
FRANK F. DREWES, *AUFGESETZT DEUTSCHE BAUZEITSCHRIFT*, JULY.
BORIS MUÑOZ, "LOT/EK," *ESTILO*, JUNE.
MAURIZIO VITTA, "CONTAINER SUL TETTO," *L'ARCA*, APRIL.
> 1996
M. LINDSAY BIERMAN, "URBAN OUTFITTERS," *INTERIOR DESIGN*,
DECEMBER.
MAYER RUS, "URBAN RENEWAL," *OUT*, (NEW YORK) OCTOBER.
MAURIZIO VITTA, "LOT/EK, IL DESIGN DEL RIFIUTO," *L'ARCA*, APRIL.
YOSHIMI MATSUO, "CUTTING EDGE OF NEW YORK," *DESIGN NEWS*
(TOKYO), SPRING.
MIKA YOSHIDA, "AMAZING SOLUTIONS," *BRUTUS*, MARCH.
> 1995
HUBERTUS RABEN, "LOT/EK," *ARCHITEKTÜR & WÖHNEN*, MAY.
> 1994
ANNALISA MILELLA, "TENDENZE," *CASA VOGUE*, SEPTEMBER.
HAMISH BOWLES, "DESIGN IN THE RAW," *VOGUE*, MAY.
BARBARA MACADAM, "FOOTLOOSE AND LOW-TECH," *ART NEWS*,
SEPTEMBER.

NICHE PADDED PLUG-IN PNEUMATIC PORTABLE POP-UP

PUSH-BUTTON RECLINABLE REVERSIBLE SELF-CONTAINED SELF-OPERATING SELF-STARTING SELF-SUPPORTING USEFUL USELESS WATERPROOF WATER RESISTANT

ACCIDENTAL ADVENTURE APPETITE ARBITRARY BY-PRODUCT CASUAL CHAIN REACTION CHALLENGE CHANCE CHAOS

COINCIDENCE CURIOUS DESIRE DISCOVER DOUBT EAGER

SI0091

SINK-WALL
STORAGE / DISPLAY / DIVIDER SYSTEM
EDIZIONI PRESS
NEW YORK 2000

EIGHTEEN 12-INCH-DEEP DOUBLE-TUB STAINLESS STEEL SINKS
ARE ASSEMBLED TO FORM TWO PIVOTING VERTICAL PANELS.

OFFICE

CONFERENCE ROOM

OFFICE

2

1

HINGED ON A CENTRAL PIVOT THE PANELS ARE USED BOTH AS
ROTATING DIVIDERS AND AS STORAGE/DISPLAY UNITS. THE BACK
OF EACH PANEL IS COATED WITH ORANGE AUTOMOTIVE PAINT
AND FINISHED WITH CLEAR RUBBER.

EMERGENCY ENCOUNTER ERROR EVENT EXPERIENTIAL EXPERIMENTAL EXPLORE HAPPEN

THE UNIQUE REQUIREMENT OF A SLOPING, CONTINUOUS CURVED SURFACE MAKES A STEEL WATER TANK THE IDEAL SHELL FOR AN INDOOR SKATEBOARD FACILITY.

THE DESIGN EXPLOITS THE CURVATURE OF THE TANK WALLS TO CONFIGURE AN INTERCONNECTED SYSTEM OF RAMPS FOR CONTINUOUS GLIDING.

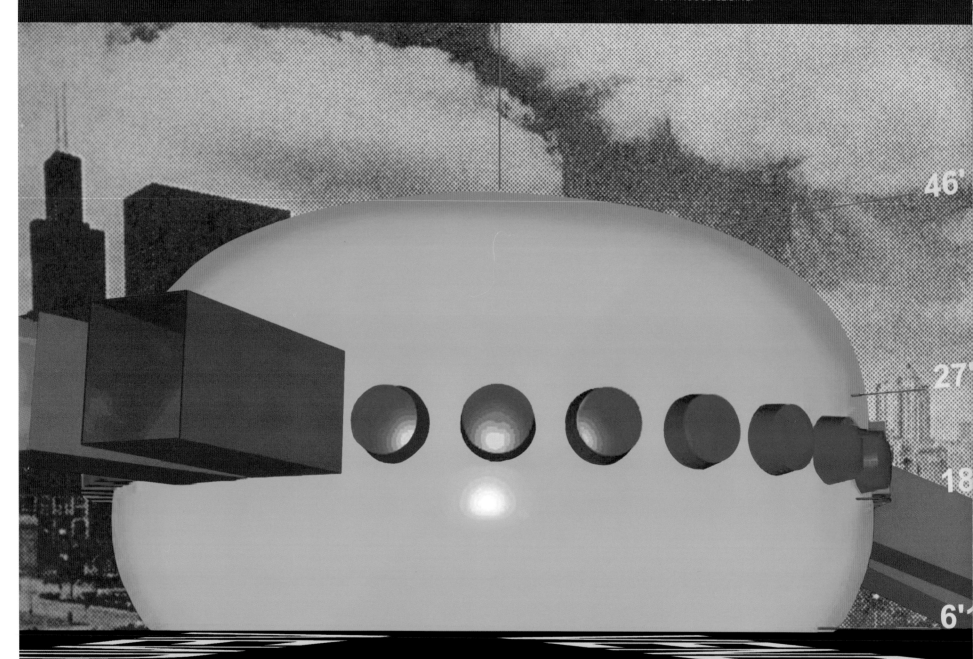

46'

27'

18'

6'1"

THE PARK IS ALSO CONCEIVED AS A PLACE FOR SOCIAL INTERACTION. THE TANK IS PLACED DIRECTLY ON THE GROUND; EXTERNAL VOLUMES PERFORATE ITS PERIMETER.

TO SATISFY FUNCTIONS OF TEENAGE GATHERING, A DENSE REPETITION OF VENDING MACHINES, LOCKERS, AND SEATING ALCOVES RUNS ALONG AN INTERIOR 360-DEGREE WALKWAY.

THE PATH IS LOCATED AT THE TOP OF THE SKATING RAMPS, AND IT IS ANIMATED BY GRAPHICS AND LIGHT. FORTY-FOOT SHIPPING CONTAINERS SERVE AS ENTRANCE AND EXIT TUNNELS; TWENTY-FOOT SHIPPING CONTAINERS HOUSE OFFICES AND BATHROOMS.

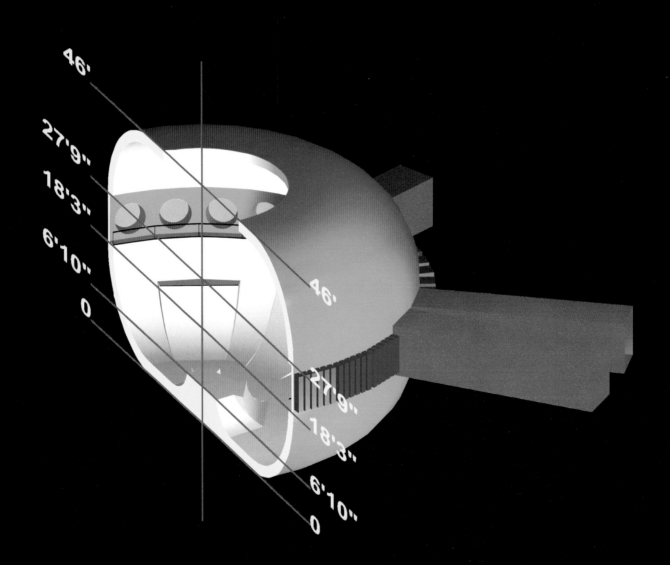

THE WHOLE INNER SURFACE OF THE TANK IS COATED WITH WHITE
EPOXY TO BE USED AS A SPHERICAL PROJECTION SCREEN,
INTRODUCING THE SKATERS INTO VIRTUAL LANDSCAPES.

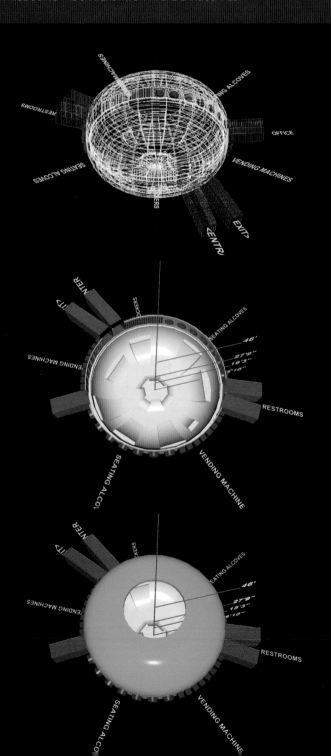

HINT IMAGINARY IMPROVISE INCIDENT INGENIOUS INSTINCT INVOLUNTARY LAPSE MISTAKE MULTIPLE CHOICE OBSESSIVE OBSTINATE OCCASION

SOUND-CHANNEL
BITSTREAMS
WHITNEY MUSEUM
NEW YORK 2001

SOUND-CHANNEL IS A LISTENING "CHANNEL" IN WHICH VISITORS
CAN RELAX BY LEANING AGAINST A DIAGONAL FOAM WALL WHILE
ENJOYING 25 DIFFERENT SOUND PIECES SELECTED FOR THE
BITSTREAMS EXHIBIT.

EACH PIECE IS ACCESSIBLE ON ITS OWN SET OF HEADPHONES CONNECTED TO A DEDICATED CD PLAYER. THE PLAYERS ARE INSERTED IN AN EXPOSED-METAL-STUD WALL FRAME PARALLEL TO THE LEANING FOAM WALL.

50 FLUORESCENT TUBES, WRAPPED IN DARK BLUE GELS, ARE ATTACHED TO THIS WALL FRAME, WHICH IS WRAPPED WITH CLEAR PLASTIC.

VISITORS ARE PARTIALLY VISIBLE AS THEY LEAN AND LISTEN, CREATING A LONG ROW OF BODIES AND GAPS THAT ECHO THE SEQUENCE OF ONES AND ZEROS THAT CONSTITUTE A "BIT STREAM."

IS AN ONGOING INVESTIGATION INTO ARTIFICIAL NATURE, OR THE UNMAPPABLE OUTGROWTH OF FAMILIAR, UNEXPLORED, MAN-MADE, AND TECHNOLOGICAL ELEMENTS WOVEN INTO URBAN AND SUBURBAN REALITY.

IS EXTRACTING FROM THIS ARTIFICIAL NATURE PREFABRICATED OBJECTS, SYSTEMS, AND TECHNOLOGIES TO BE USED AS RAW MATERIALS.

IS THE RANDOM ENCOUNTER WITH OBJECTS THAT ARE DISPLACED, TRANSFORMED, AND MANIPULATED TO FULFILL PROGRAM NEEDS.

IS THE DIALOGUE THAT DEVELOPS BETWEEN THE SPECIFIC FEATURES OF THESE EXISTING OBJECTS AND GENERATES UNEXPECTED SPATIAL AND FUNCTIONAL SOLUTIONS.

IS RETHINKING THE WAYS IN WHICH THE HUMAN BODY INTERACTS WITH PRODUCTS AND BY-PRODUCTS OF INDUSTRIAL / TECHNOLOGICAL CULTURE.

IS RE-INVENTING DOMESTIC, WORK, AND PLAY SPACES AND FUNCTIONS, AND QUESTIONING CONVENTIONAL CONFIGURATIONS.

IS BLURRING THE BOUNDARIES BETWEEN ART, ARCHITECTURE, ENTERTAINMENT, AND INFORMATION.

IS AN ARCHITECTURE STUDIO BASED IN NEW YORK.

STUDENT PAVILION
MULTIFUNCTIONAL SPACE
UNIVERSITY OF WASHINGTON SEATTLE 2000

A 60-FOOT-LONG SECTION, CUT OUT BETWEEN THE MAIN WINGS
AND THE TAIL OF A BOEING 747 FUSELAGE, IS PLACED ON A
SLOPING SITE ON THE UNIVERSITY CAMPUS OVERLOOKING LAKE
UNION.

ON SITE, THE FUSELAGE IS HELD MIDAIR ON A STEEL PIPE CRADLE. A STEEL RAMP ALLOWS ACCESS TO ITS INTERIOR SPACE. INSIDE, THE AIRPLANE SECTION IS STRIPPED DOWN TO REVEAL ITS INTRICATE ALUMINUM RIB CAGE.

THE FLOORING ON THE MAIN DECK IS SUBSTITUTED WITH METAL GRATING FILLED WITH CLEAR RESIN, AND WITH A ROTATING FLOOR / SEATING SYSTEM THAT TAKES ADVANTAGE OF THE LOWER FREIGHT HOLD.

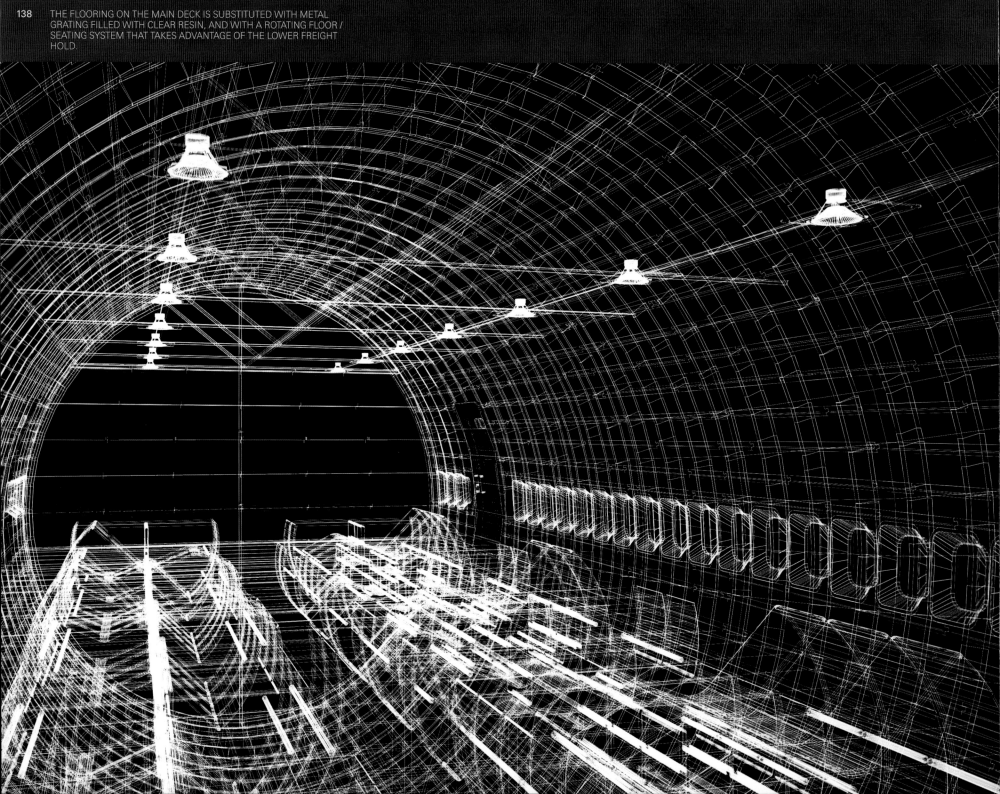

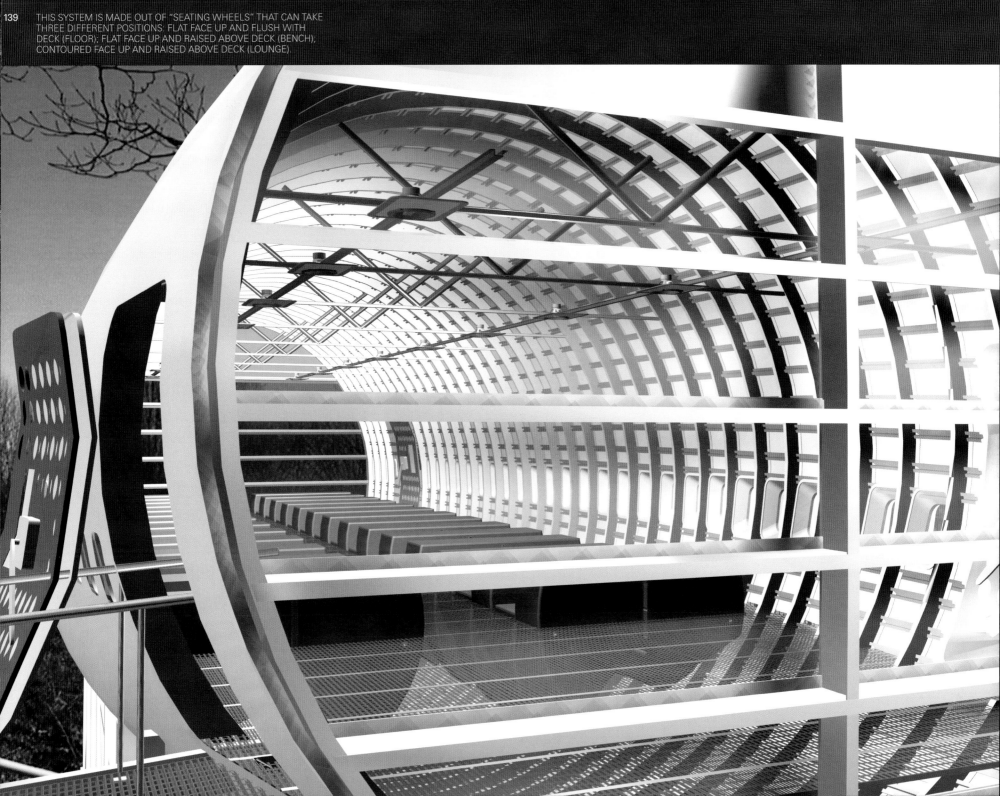

THIS SYSTEM IS MADE OUT OF "SEATING WHEELS" THAT CAN TAKE
THREE DIFFERENT POSITIONS: FLAT FACE UP AND FLUSH WITH
DECK (FLOOR); FLAT FACE UP AND RAISED ABOVE DECK (BENCH);
CONTOURED FACE UP AND RAISED ABOVE DECK (LOUNGE).

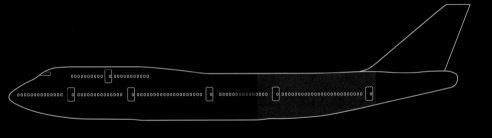

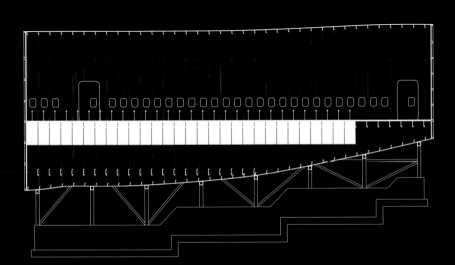

BY ROTATING AND/OR LIFTING THESE "WHEELS" THE INTERIOR
OF THE FUSELAGE CAN BE SET UP IN MULTIPLE CONFIGURATIONS TO
BE USED FOR DIFFERENT EVENTS: LECTURES, SCREENINGS,
PERFORMANCES, PARTIES, LOUNGING.

PROJECTION SCREENS LINE THE PERIMETER OF THE FUSELAGE.
INTERNET CONNECTIVITY AND AC POWER SUPPLY ARE PROVIDED
AT ALL SEATS.

SURF-A-BED
MULTISCREEN CHANNEL SURFING SYSTEM
HENRY URBACH ARCHITECTURE GALLERY
NEW YORK 1997

A HOVERING PLANE OF TELEVISION LIGHT AND IMAGERY, SUSPENDED OVER A BED, EXPLORES THE POTENTIAL FOR IMAGE SCRAMBLING AND REPETITION.

TELEVISION IMAGES DRAWN FROM ALL AVAILABLE SOURCES— CABLE TV, VCRS, SURVEILLANCE CAMERAS—ARE BROADCASTED SIMULTANEOUSLY.

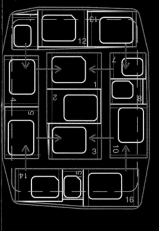

RUBBER BINDING

REFLECTED CEILING PLAN

CEILING HOOKS LAYOUT

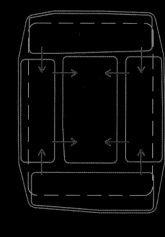

STEEL CABLES

RUBBER BINDING

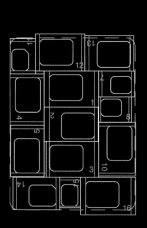

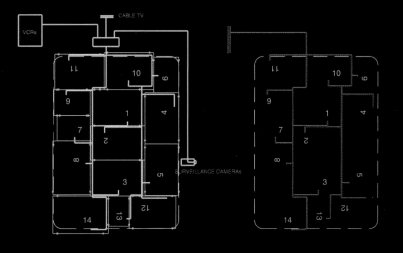

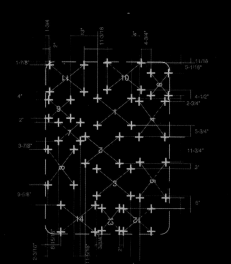

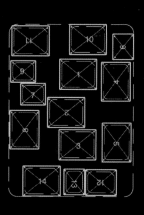

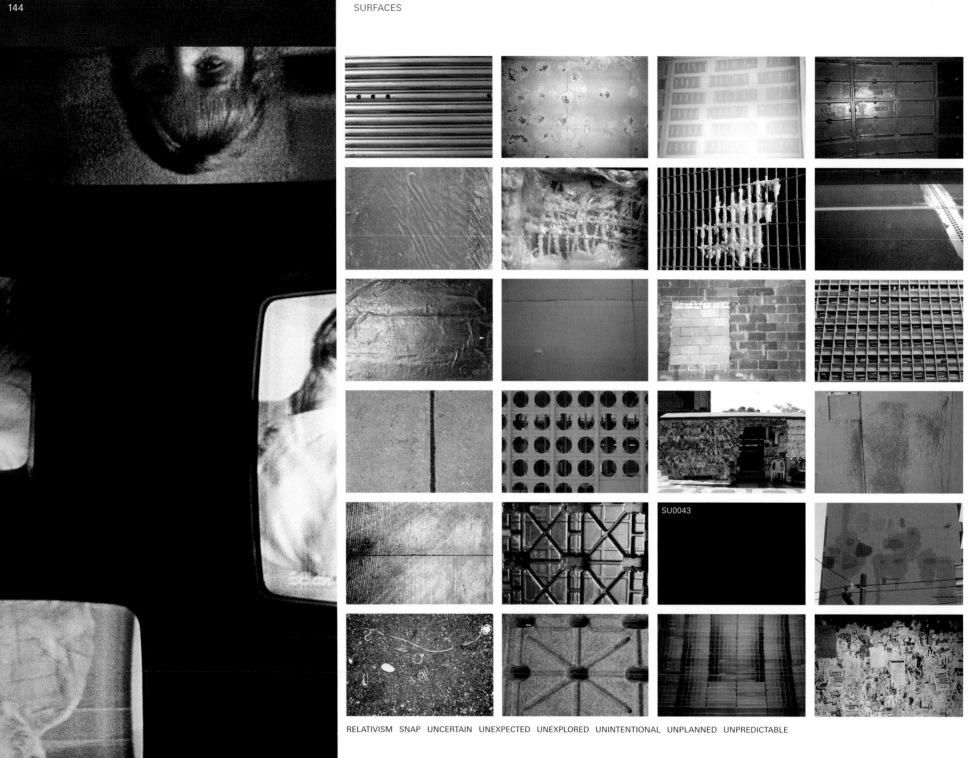

SU0043

RELATIVISM SNAP UNCERTAIN UNEXPECTED UNEXPLORED UNINTENTIONAL UNPLANNED UNPREDICTABLE

UNPREMEDITATED

SV0045

SV0046

SV0047

IMG 000

ACENTRIC ANTIGRAVITY ANTITHESIS ASLANT ASYMMETRIC CONTRADICT CONTRARY COUNTERCLOCKWISE CROOKED DARE DECENTRALIZE DEFY DEFICIENT

DEREGULATE DESPITE DISCORDANCE DISESTABLISH DISPROPORTIONATE DISREGARD ILLEGAL ILLEGITIMATE ILLICIT ILLOGICAL IMPERTINENT

INAPPROPRIATE INCORRECT INDECENT IMPERFECT IMPRECISE IMPURE INADEQUATE INCOHERENT

INACCURATE INSUFFICIENT IRREGULAR LIMP OBLIQUE SUBVERT TILTED UNBALANCED UNEQUAL UNEVEN UNSTABLE VERTIGO

TN0032

TN0004

TN0033

TN0034

TN0004

ACTIVATE ADDICT AFFECT AGITATE AMAZE AMUSING ANIMATE APPEAL ATTRACT CAPTIVATE CAPTURE COMPEL DRIVE ENGAGE

ENGAGING ENTERTAIN EXCITE EXPLOIT FUNNY HOOKED IMPACT IMPEL INDUCE INFLUENCE INITIATE INSTIGATE

INTERROGATIVE INTRIGUE LAUNCH MOTIVATE PRESSURE PROMPT PROVOKE PUSH SPUR STIMULATE SURPRISE TRIGGER URGE

TR0078

TR0087

TR0088

ADAPT ALIENATE APPROPRIATE ASSOCIATE BORROW COMMUTE CONVERT DERIVATION DERIVATIVE

DISASSOCIATE DISCONNECT DISPLACE ESTRANGE

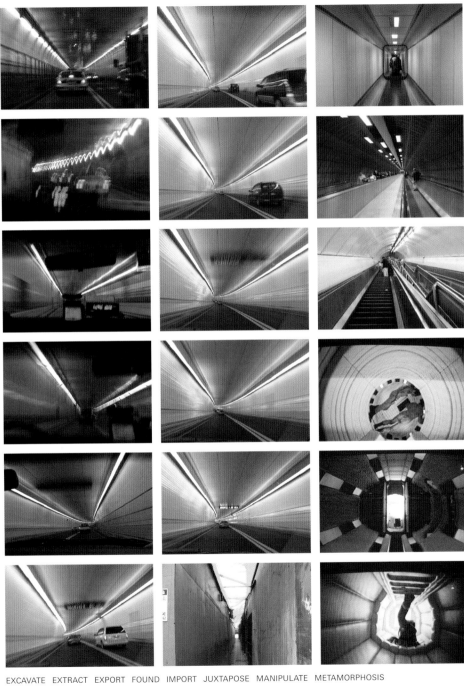

EXCAVATE EXTRACT EXPORT FOUND IMPORT JUXTAPOSE MANIPULATE METAMORPHOSIS

TV-LITE
TELEVISION LIGHTING SYSTEM
HENRY URBACH ARCHITECTURE GALLERY
NEW YORK 1997

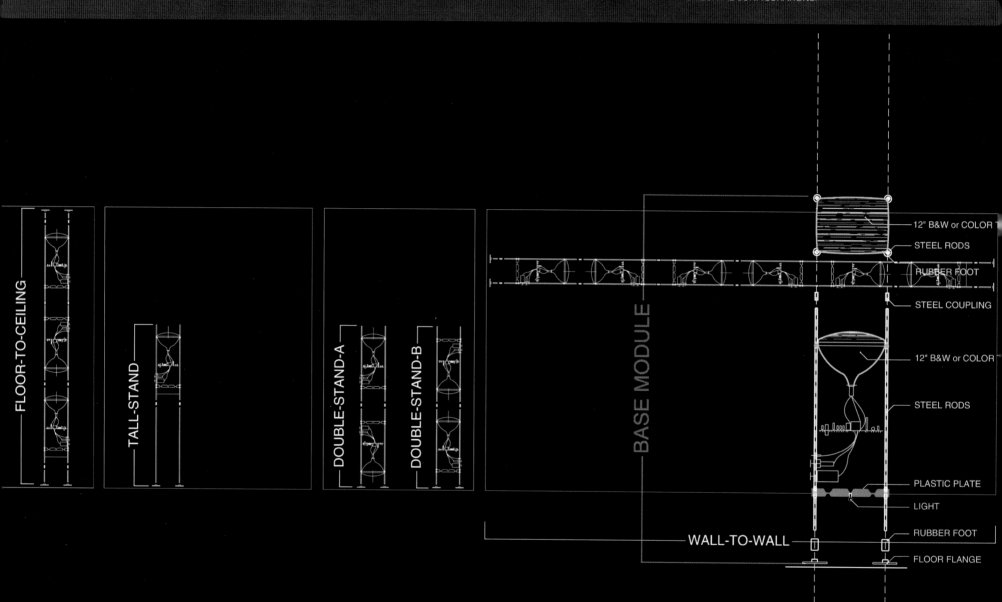

FLOOR-TO-CEILING

TALL-STAND

DOUBLE-STAND-A

DOUBLE-STAND-B

BASE MODULE

12" B&W or COLOR

STEEL RODS

RUBBER FOOT

STEEL COUPLING

12" B&W or COLOR

STEEL RODS

PLASTIC PLATE

LIGHT

RUBBER FOOT

FLOOR FLANGE

WALL-TO-WALL

MIGRATE MISAPPROPRIATE MODIFY MUTATE MUTANT PERMUTE

RECONFIGURE REMOVE RENAME REPLACE RETHINK REUSE REVERSE SHIFT STRANGER TRANSFER TRANSMUTATION TRANSFORM

TV-TANK TRANSFORMS A PETROLEUM TRAILER TANK INTO A SET
OF FLOATING SECTIONS SUITABLE FOR LOUNGING AND WATCHING
TELEVISION.

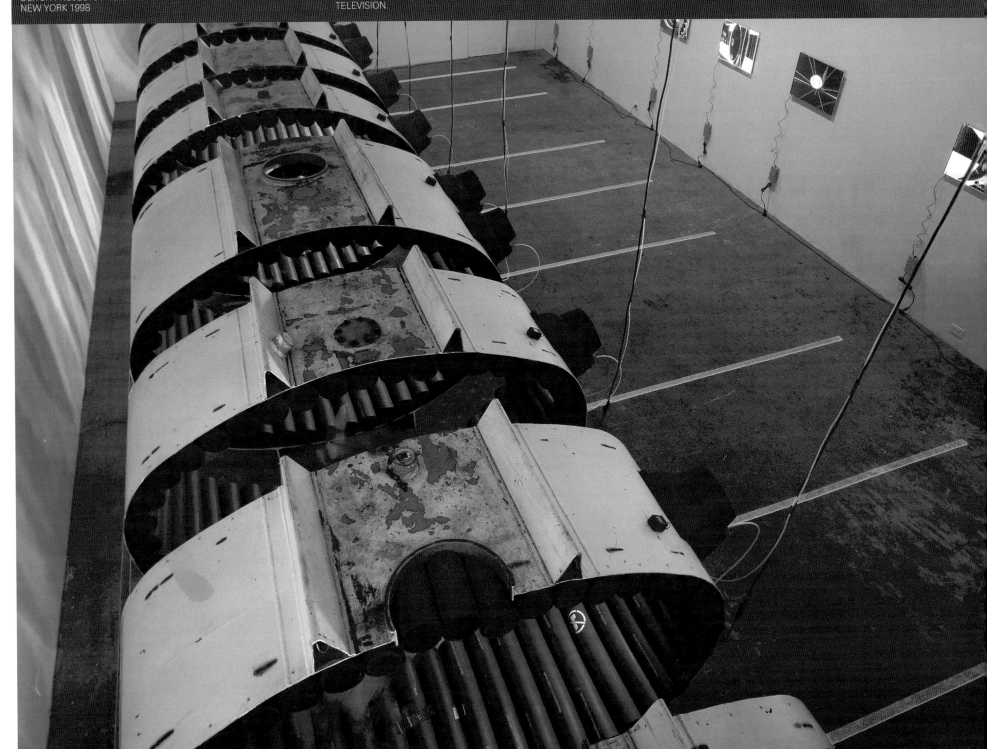

THE 35-FOOT-LONG ALUMINUM TANK IS SLICED INTO EIGHT RINGS.
EACH SECTION IS LINED WITH RUBBER TUBING AND EQUIPPED WITH
CABLE TV AND REMOTE CONTROL.

VIEWERS LOUNGE IN THE PRIVACY OF SINGLE OR DOUBLE
SECTIONS, WHILE EXPERIENCING THE ONCE-HIDDEN INTERIOR
OF THE ENTIRE OIL TANK, NOW ANIMATED BY THE FLICKER
OF TELEVISION LIGHT.
SECTIONS CAN BE EXTRACTED TO BECOME INDIVIDUAL VIEWING
MODULES.

2020 Hindsight / Philip Nobel

> When did it happen that the last connection was made to the last free building, to the last free-floating floor, to at last link all and each and every one to everything else? When did that last I-beam cross that last unbridged street, its charge of wires and pipes slung below like an infant, linking with its twin to bring a halt to the progress of the city's creeping sinews? There is no more getting away from it all by getting above it. There is no more bird's-eye view, no terrace or sky-deck where the sounds of the trickling waters (gray goes up, black goes down) and the ring of live wires won't intrude—where the call of train brakes fade in a moment of repose, the engineer thinking of his fresh water trucked in that morning from the sea. (The tubes of the Third Water Tunnel were finished just in time. They were taken over by the desalination plant. Water was pumped through them, uphill. Then they caved in.) Here it seems that the whole city has become an iron lung. Each citizen allotted a ration of air and light, amounts to be adjusted monthly on a survey polybagged with the cable bill. And everyone is happy.

> The surface is contested, the subsurface is lost: go up. For the most part it was a peaceful process, each building colonized in the night by the tubes and fibers of its next-door neighbor. And on and on, back to the central hubs, windowless exchanges set up at the mercy of real estate and the favor of local pols, looking the other way. There were some hold outs. Downtown, east and west, despite its history of catacombs, was reluctant to join in the encroaching union. Some there looked back to a time when buildings were built piece-meal, unplugged, and they rallied around the memory. But they got theirs. One core began at the Holland Tunnel—its outboard ventilator was co-opted to move breathable air—and grew, despite protest, to comprise the whole flank of the island, following the track of the old High Line. (There were farms here once, and warehouses.)

> It deformed to the Archives as if to an ancient tell, incorporated the southernmost stand of the West Village, carried the unconsumed row houses as a glacier carries a stone. It is said that one can see the lump of a devoured but undigested Doric portico moving toward the river in a section of the purging structure (Muni P5) that runs along the line of old Charles Lane.

> In other areas of the city, the changes were hardly resisted. In Midtown, where, as now, only the eccentric lived, and where the germ of the new growth was long ago planted under the eyes of Prometheus at the foot of 30 Rock, it was business as usual. There, too,

the street-level citizens would savor the new historicity of their original urban hives: Grand Central, on- and off-limits, the abandoned malls that entwine themselves around skyscraper piers, or—more than any other place looking forward to the call of the coming order—the tunnels and tombs of the Times Square subway station. (They tried to renovate it once.) In Times Square, as early as the twentieth century, before the roof, the presses and trains together tried to shake the sleeping city awake, a new thing was being born right there. Its flower—can a plant flower without stress?—is the vertical core of the Marriott Marquis (though the architect himself did not know it and played no role.) Behind the theaters, too—Theaters!—while the audiences were otherwise detained, the buildings felt out for each other. Could anyone hear it? The sound of the fire stairs, black rails and silver ducts, later steel and brick, stretching to connect would not compete with the orchestra in the pit. Or applause. And where did these people go? They went out, still blind, to the racks that held their cars and drove away into the corrupted grid, never as regular as we are told it used to be.

> Look at it: once so straight, so uniform, they say. Forgetting errant Broadway, that necessary deviant, what of the one-notch alleys, the pipes laid at angles to the curb, the chamfered storefront corners, the braces on construction decks, cabs out of line, the wavering of curtain walls, the affront of leaning trees, mismeasurement, ferry wakes, faults? What of the busses that pull away into traffic and remain too long out of true? How did this go unnoticed? How did it happen that there was any surprise at all when the last building connected touched the last building left exposed? And how did people live before, in the open, so alone under the sky without the comforts of the city?

TRANSPOSE UPDATE

VERTICAL LEISURE CENTER (COMPETITION)
TEMPORARY STRUCTURE AT PS1
NEW YORK 2000

A THREE-LEVEL METAL SCAFFOLD IS POSITIONED ACROSS THE
COURTYARD OF THE PS1 ARTS CENTER.

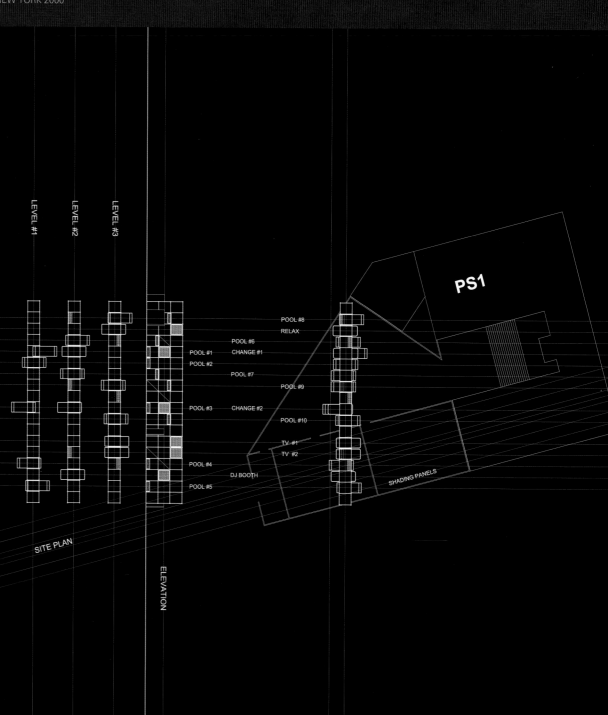

THE SCAFFOLD HOLDS A VERTICAL LEISURE CENTER TO BE USED BY
VISITORS DURING THE SUMMER AS A CONTEMPORARY "LOGGIA"
FOR THE ENJOYMENT OF SUN, SHADE, WATER, CITY VIEWS, SOUND,
AND MOVING IMAGE.

THE STRUCTURE EMERGES ABOVE THE BOUNDARY WALLS OF THE
COURTYARD SO THAT IT IS VISIBLE FROM THE STREET.

SHIPPING CONTAINERS ARE ALSO INSERTED INTO THE SCAFFOLDING TO HOUSE CHANGING ROOMS, A DJ BOOTH, TV LOUNGES, AND REFRESHMENT SHOPS.

A DENSE PLASTIC MESH IS STRETCHED ALONG THE TOP AND SIDES OF THE STRUCTURE TO PROVIDE SHADE.

SUNBATHING AND SHADED REST AREAS ALTERNATE ALONG THE WALKS THROUGHOUT THE LENGTH OF THE SCAFFOLD AT TWO DIFFERENT LEVELS.

VISION-TUBE
PROPOSAL FOR THE WHITNEY BIENNIAL
NEW YORK 2000

VISION-TUBE IS A DEVICE FOR URBAN MONITORING. IT IS AN
ELEVATED TUNNEL BEARING SURVEILLANCE CAMERAS INSERTED
INTO THE CHANNEL GARDEN AT ROCKEFELLER CENTER.

AT FIFTH AVENUE, A RAMP INVITES VISITORS INTO THE SPACE.
THE HOVERING TUNNEL CONTAINS A PATH FITTED WITH VISION
AND PERCEPTION DEVICES.

SURVEILLANCE CAMERAS, ATTACHED TO STEEL APPENDAGES LOCATED ON THE OUTER SKIN OF THE TUBE, SURVEY LIFE AND ZOOM IN ON THE SURROUNDING STREETS, OFFICES, STORES, AND ON THE RINK.

PROJECTORS REVEAL THEIR VIEWS ONTO THE CURVED INNER WALLS OF THE TUBE. VISITORS ALONG THIS NEW URBAN PATH WITNESS A SAMPLER OF EVERYDAY ACTIONS SELECTED BY THE TUBE'S MANY EYES.

THE PROJECTED SCENES BECOME THE ONLY REFERENCE AS THE TUBE RISES HIGHER ABOVE THE GARDEN, CULMINATING ABOVE THE RINK.

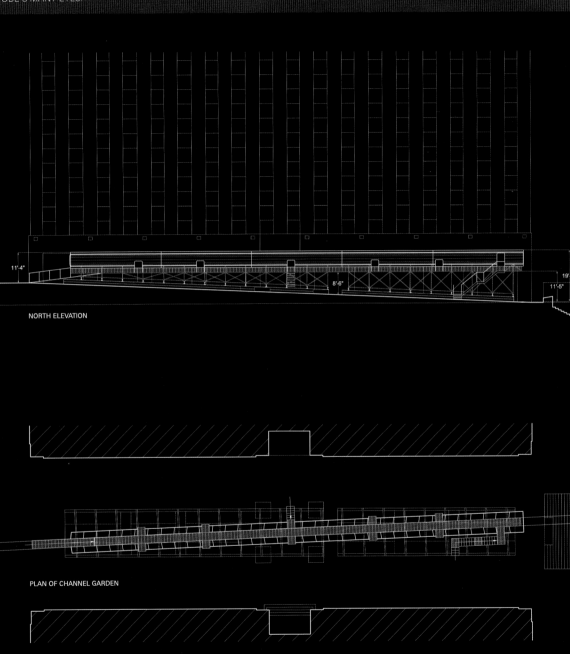

NORTH ELEVATION

PLAN OF CHANNEL GARDEN

VISION-TUBE IS COMPOSED OF SIX ALUMINUM GASOLINE TANKS
JOINED INTO A CONTINUOUS 210-FOOT-LONG SPACE PARTED BY
THE TANKS' BAFFLE WALLS, THROUGH WHICH DOORWAYS HAVE
BEEN CUT.

THE TANKS' BOTTOMS HAVE ALSO BEEN CUT, AND VISITORS WALK ON A LOWER CATWALK WITH ONLY THEIR UPPER BODIES INSIDE THE TUBE.

A STEEL SCAFFOLD THAT RISES ABOVE THE CHANNEL GARDEN SUPPORTS THE TANKS AND CATWALKS. AT ITS HIGHEST, THE CATWALK RETURNS VISITORS TO THE PLAZA THROUGH A STAIRCASE RUNNING ALONG THE ICE RINK.

THE EXISTING POOLS AND PLANTERS DISAPPEAR UNDER A MOUND OF SAND.

AGGLOMERATE COEXIST CONFUSION CONGESTION COHABIT CONURBATION COSMOPOLIS CROWD DENSITY DISORDER

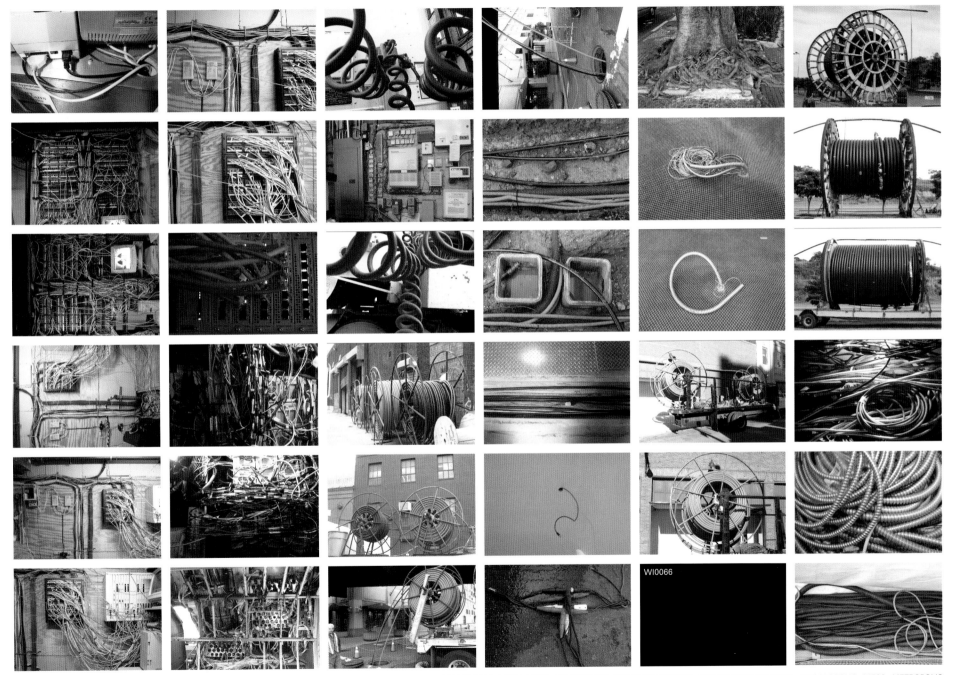

DISORIENT ENDLESS ENORMOUS EXCHANGE INTERACT INTERCONNECT LOUD MASS MASS-MEDIA MASS-PRODUCTION MASS-TRANSPORTATION MEGALOPOLIS MESS METROPOLIS

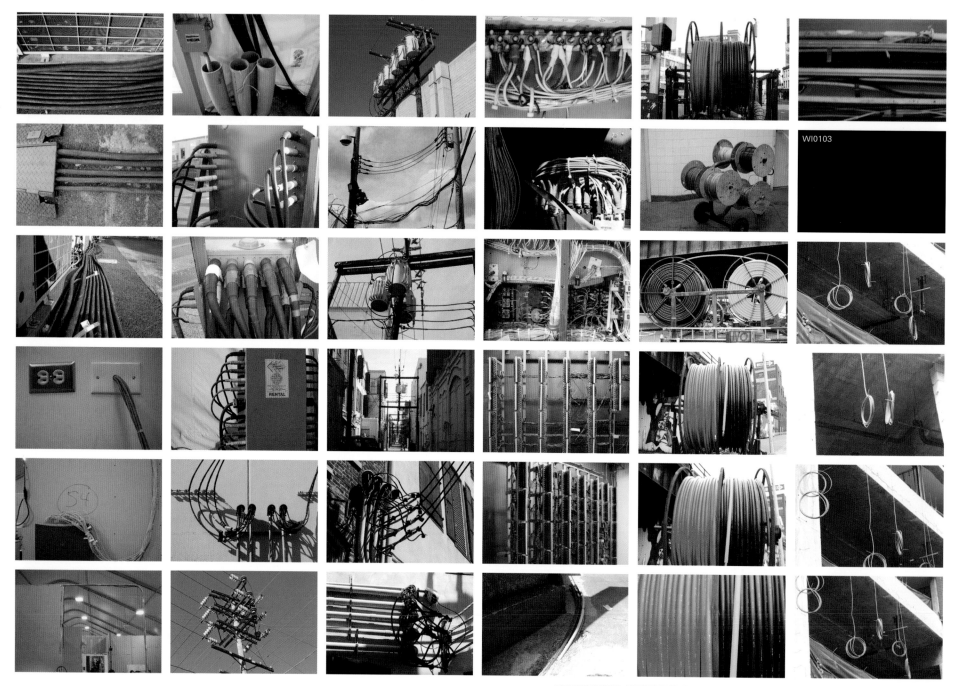

WI0103

MULTICENTERED   MULTICOLORED   MULTICULTURAL   MULTIETHNIC   MULTIFORM   MULTILAYERED